# Britain 1815-51

# Britain 1815-51

Design by John Rushton Associates
Picture research by Procaudio Ltd

Maps by Tim Smith


Holmes McDougall Ltd, Allander House,
137-141 Leith Walk, Edinburgh EH6 8NS

SBN 7157 1567 - 4

**Project team**

David Sylvester (Director to 1975)
Tony Boddington (Director from 1975)
Gwenifer Griffiths (1975-1976)
William Harrison (1972-1975)
John Mann (1974-1975)
Aileen Plummer (from 1972)
Denis Shemilt (Evaluator from 1974)
Peter Wenham (1972-1974)

Printed in Great Britain by
Holmes McDougall Ltd, Edinburgh

**Acknowledgements**

Thanks are extended to Tom Scherb
(Gosforth High School), Eric Magee (John
Wilmott School, Sutton Coldfield) and
David Blackburn (Kimbolton School) who
helped with the early stages of this study
at the 1975 Leeds Writing Conference.
Alan Heeson of Durham University also
gave invaluable advice about sources and
picture research for the case study on
The Sunderland By-election.

# Contents

## 1 The Vote
page 7

## 2 The Poor
page 47

**Emigration after 1815 A case study**
page 78

## 3 The Church and Social Reform
page 95

## 4 Railways
page 119

## 5 Broadsides and Ballads
page 153

# 1
# The Vote

OPPOSITE: In 1815, rapidly growing cities such as Leeds (shown here) were unrepresented in Parliament

## After the war

In 1815, Britain was at peace for the first time in over twenty years. During the war period (1793-1815), the main issue had been survival in the war with France. But once the war ended, both old and new problems received more attention (source 1).

A trade depression made poverty and unemployment worse than ever; and it seemed that those least able to look after themselves came off worst. For example, the Government decided to use the Corn Laws to protect farmers from renewed foreign competition once the war was over. Those who suffered most as a result—the poor and the unemployed who had to buy bread at artificially high prices—protested in desperation.

Rich and powerful landowners controlled Parliament at this time and were able to protect their own interests. And they controlled Parliament because they had no opposition; the majority of people had no say in government because they had no vote. Despite the fear of change, it was clear that this situation could not last for ever. Once the war was over, demands for parliamentary reform grew stronger (sources 2, 3).

During the period we are studying, some changes did occur, and even where people were unsuccessful in bringing about change, the ground was prepared for reforms later on. Even so, by 1851, many men were still unenfranchised, and no women were allowed to vote.

The following sections tell the story of what happened.

RIGHT: A satirical comment on society from a contemporary cartoonist. In an age before radio, film and television, cartoons had important propaganda uses

STATE OF THE NATION.

ABOVE: Samuel Bamford, author of
*Passages in the Life of a Radical*

RIGHT: Three borough constituencies.
They offer an interesting comparison
with the picture of Leeds on page 6

## SOURCE 1 After the war, 1815

The war, which began in 1793, is now over. The troops are not all come home, the
ships are not all paid off, the account is not wound up; but the war is over. Social
Order is restored; the French are again in the power of the Bourbons; the Revolution
is at an end; no change has been effected in England; our Boroughs, and our Church,
and Nobility and all have been preserved; our government tells us, that we have
covered ourselves with glory.

William Cobbett, *Weekly Political Register*, 25 September 1815

## SOURCE 2 Unrest at the end of the war—the author was himself arrested at Peterloo as one of the speakers

A series of disturbances commenced with the introduction of the Corn Bill in 1815,
and continued with short intervals, until the close of the year 1816. In London and
Westminster riots ensued, and were continued for several days, whilst the Bill was discussed; at Bridport, there were riots on account of the high price of bread; at Bidde-
ford there were similar disturbances to prevent the exportation of grain; at Bury, by
the unemployed, to destroy machinery; at Ely, not suppressed without bloodshed;
at Newcastle-on-Tyne, by colliers and others; at Glasgow, where blood was shed, on
account of the soup kitchens; at Preston, by unemployed weavers; at Nottingham by
Luddites who destroyed thirty frames; at Merthyr Tydville, on a reduction of wages;
at Birmingham, by the unemployed; at Walsall, by the distressed; and . . . at Dundee,
where owing to the high price of meal, upwards of one hundred shops were
plundered.

Samuel Bamford, *Passages in the Life of a Radical*, Simpkin, 1844, Vol. III, pp. 6–7

## SOURCE 3 Paying taxes and the vote

We have seen that the cause of our miseries is the burden of taxes occasioned by wars,
by standing armies, by sinecures, by pensions etc. the remedy is what we have now to
look to, and that remedy consists wholly and solely of such a reform in the Commons
or People's House of Parliament, as shall give to every payer of direct taxes a vote at
elections, and as shall cause the Members to be elected annually.

'An Address to the Journeymen and Labourers', in Cobbett's *Weekly Political Register*,
2 November 1816

## Who voted?

Before the Reform Act of 1832, many people had no right to vote in elections. Women were not allowed to vote, except in special cases, and many large centres of population had no separate Members of Parliament. On the other hand, some places of no importance had the power to return Members of Parliament. Appleby in Cumbria for example had only one elector, and whoever won his vote became an MP! (sources 4, 27).

Reformers called places like Appleby 'rotten boroughs'—the electorate was so small that the bribery of a handful of voters was enough to gain a seat in the House of Commons.

In elections for parliamentary seats to represent a county, all men who owned property worth forty shillings a year were allowed to vote. However, in the borough elections the franchise varied from one place to another (source 5).

This explains why in some places the electorate might be so few in number. In some boroughs, wealthy landowners and aristocrats controlled voters. This could happen when the elector was employed by or lived in a house owned by an influential man. These boroughs were called 'pocket boroughs'. Contemporaries recognised that it was difficult to run a government without the goodwill of the aristocracy (source 6).

The Mirror

OF

LITERATURE, AMUSEMENT, AND INSTRUCTION.

No. 492.]          SATURDAY, JUNE 4, 1831.          [PRICE 2d.

THREE BOROUGHS

*Proposed to be wholly disfranchised by the* REFORM BILL.

1. DUNWICH.          2. OLD SARUM.          3. BRAMBER.

ABOVE: A local newspaper advertises votes for sale by means of buying six cottages

## SOURCE 4 Sir Philip Francis, MP for Appleby and reformer, describes 'How to become an MP'

I was unanimously elected by one elector to represent this ancient borough in Parliament . . . there was no other Candidate, no Opposition, no Poll demanded . . . so I had nothing to do but to thank the said Elector for the Unanimous Voice with which I was chosen . . . On Friday morning I shall quit this triumphant scene with flying colours and a noble determination not to see it again in less than seven years.

*Francis Letters*, Vol. II, p. 493 in Julius West, *A History of the Chartist Movement*, Constable, 1920, p. 14

## SOURCE 5 The qualifications to vote in the boroughs before 1832

Your committee will now call your attention to the various rights of voting in the different places returning Members of Parliament . . .

With respect to the different cities, towns, and boroughs, they exercise a variety of separate and distinct rights, . . . In the greater part of them . . . the right of voting appears to be vested in the freemen . . . but . . . an infinite diversity of peculiar customs is to be found. In some places the number of voters is limited to a select body not exceeding 30 or 40; in others it is extended to 8 [000] or 10 000. In some places the freeman must be a resident inhabitant to entitle him to vote; in others his presence is only required at an election. The right to the freedom is also different in different boroughs . . .

The remaining rights of voting are of a still more complicated description. Burgage-holds, leaseholds, and freeholds,—scot and lot, inhabitants householders, inhabitants at large, potwallopers, and commonalty, each in different boroughs prevail, and create endless misunderstandings, from the difficulty which is daily found to arise in defining and settling those numerous distinctions, . . .

*Report of the Society of the Friends of the People*, 9 February 1793

## SOURCE 6 The influence of the aristocracy: Mr Croker to George Canning, 3 April 1827

I think it right to send you a memorandum which will show you, in one view, how impossible it is to do anything satisfactory towards a Government in this country

without the help of the aristocracy. I know that you must be well aware of this, yet the following summary may not be useless to you, though I know that it is imperfect.

Numbers of members returned to the House of Commons by the influence of some of the peers:

*Tories*—Lord Lonsdale 9, Lord Hertford 8, Duke of Rutland 6, Duke of Newcastle 5, Lord Yarborough (for W Holmes) 5, Lord Powis 4, Lord Falmouth 4, Lord Anglesey 4, Lord Ailesbury 4, Lord Radnor 3, Duke of Northumberland 4, Duke of Buccleugh 4, Marquess of Stafford 3, Duke of Buckingham (2) 3 (sic), Lord Mount-Edgcumbe 4—(total) 70; besides at least 12 or 14 who have each two seats, say 26—(total) 96.

*Whigs*—Lord Fitzwilliam 8, Lord Darlington 7, Duke of Devonshire 7, Duke of Norfolk 6, Lord Grosvenor 6, Duke of Bedford 4, Lord Carrington 4—(total) 42; with about half a dozen who have each a couple of seats 12—(total) 54.

L. J. Jennings (ed), *Correspondence and Diaries of John Wilson Croker*, Vol. 1, London, 1884, p. 73

ABOVE RIGHT: A candidate tries to win a vote by flattery. 'My dear Mrs Perkins', he is saying, 'so happy to see you, how are all your sweet dear darling children—your eldest daughter blooming like a rose—might I ask you to use your influence with your worthy husband—allow me to kiss that fair hand'

ABOVE LEFT: A show of hands for a Liberal candidate, as the candidate distributes 50 000 reasons for being elected

ABOVE: A Phiz cartoon from *Pickwick Papers* gives a commonly held view of electioneering. As can be seen in the Case Study about the Sunderland By-election of 1841, political issues were discussed, but as that study also shows, election results often depended on non-political issues

RIGHT: An election ball. Apart from any profit to be made from selling votes, elections were welcomed because they were social occasions

# Elections

Both before and after the 1832 Reform Act, contested elections were very expensive for candidates. The 1808 Lincoln election, for example, is said to have cost £25 000. Support had to be bought. This might mean paying money to a person who controlled a 'pocket borough', or buying people's votes.

Many electors saw their vote as personal property—something which they could sell to the highest bidder. In Boston a vote cost five guineas; in Wallingford it cost forty guineas (sources 7, 8). Then there was 'treating': support was bought by means of giving electors a good time. This could simply mean buying plenty of beer, or it might mean putting on a special election banquet (source 9). The votes of tradesmen could be bought by putting business their way at election time.

The amount of money changing hands during elections often made them violent and drunken occasions. And men could be hired to intimidate supporters of a rival candidate. In the case of the East Retford election, the military were used to end the violence. When the result was known, the House of Commons declared it void because the election had been so corrupt (sources 10, 11).

## SOURCE 7 Vote selling in Athlone

My native town was neither better nor worse than most of the Irish and English constituencies of the time. Its distinction was that the number of voters was small and that, therefore, the amount of the bribe was high. The bribe averaged £30 or £40 the vote; and there were tales of a vote having run up to £100 in one of Keogh's elections. With many of the people the periodic bribe entered into the whole economy of their squalid and weary lives. Men continued to live in houses who had better have lived in lodgings because the house gave them the vote.

T. P. O'Connor, *Memoirs*, Benn, 1929, Vol. I, p. 380


## SOURCE 8 Corruption back-fires

To the intense disgust of the majority of the electors, I refused to bribe at all, announcing my determination to 'stand on patriotic principles' which, in the electioneering parlance of those days, meant 'no bribery'. To my astonishment, however, a considerable number of the respectable inhabitants voted in my favour . . .

Having had decisive proof as to the nature of Honiton politics, I made up my mind that the next time there was a vacancy in the borough, the seat should be mine without bribery. Accordingly, immediately after my defeat, I sent the bellman round the town, having first primed him with an appropriate speech, intimating that 'all who had voted for me, might repair to my agent, J. Townend Esq., and receive ten pounds ten!'

The novelty of a defeated candidate paying double the current price expended by the successful one—or, indeed, paying anything—made a great sensation . . . The impression produced was simply this—that if I gave ten guineas for being beaten, my opponent had not paid half enough for being elected; . . .

The result was what had been foreseen. My opponent, though successful, was regarded with anything but a favourable eye; I, though defeated, had suddenly become most popular. The effect at the next election, must be reserved for its place in a future chapter . . .

[In the following July, another election was held.]

ABOVE: Thomas Cochrane, Earl of Dundonald

No time was lost in proceeding to Honiton, where considerable sensation was created by my entrance into the town in a vis-à-vis and six, followed by several carriages and four filled with officers and seamen of the *Pallas*, who volunteered to accompany me on the occasion.

Our reception by the townspeople was enthusiastic, the more so, perhaps, from the general belief that my capture of the Spanish galleons—as they were termed—had endowed me with untold wealth; whilst an equally fabulous amount was believed to have resulted from our recent cruise . . .

Aware of my previous objection to bribery, not a word was asked by my partisans, as to the price expected in exchange for their suffrages. It was enough that my former friends had received ten guineas each after my defeat, and it was judged best to leave the cost of success to my discretion.

My return was triumphant, and it was then plainly asked, what consideration was to be expected by those who had supported me in so delicate a manner.

'Not one farthing!' was the reply.

'But, my lord, you gave ten guineas a head to the minority at the last election, and the majority have been calculating on something handsome on the present occasion.'

'No doubt. The former gift was for their conduct in not taking the bribe of five pounds from the agents of my opponent. For me now to pay them would be a violation of my own previously expressed principles.'

Thomas Cochrane, Earl of Dundonald, *Autobiography of a Seaman*, London, 1861, pp. 179-181, 202-3

### SOURCE 9 The cost of treating

The permission thus given [to give his constituents a public supper] was converted into a public treat; not only for my partisans, but for my opponents, their wives, children and friends; in short for the whole town! The result showed itself in a bill for some twelve hundred pounds!

Cochrane, *Autobiography of a Seaman*, p. 204

## SOURCE 10 Election day—A sketch from nature

### The Hustings

Now, hail ye, groans, huzzas, and cheers,
So grateful to electors' ears,
Where all is riot and confusion,
Fraud, friendship, scandal and delusion;
Now houses stormed and windows broken,
Serve as a pastime and a token
That patriots spare not, in their zeal
Such measures for their country's weal.
Now greeting, hooting and abuse,
To each man's party prove of use;
And mud, and stones, and waving hats,
And broken heads and putrid cats,
Are offerings made to aid the cause
Of order, government and laws,
Now lampoons, idle tales and jokes,
And placards overreach and hoax;
While blustering, bullying, and brow-beating,
A little pomeling and maltreating,
And elbowing, jostling and cajoling,
And all the jockey ship of polling,
And deep manoeuvre and duplicity,
Prove all elections fair and free.

Anonymous

## SOURCE 11 The East Retford election, 1826: Lord Fitzwilliam, a wealthy Whig nobleman, gives his own fairly objective view

. . . The riot Act has been twice read already and the civil power is quite set at defiance. The constables have been struck and their staffs taken from them . . . Some men have been nearly killed by a hired mob of the scum of the neighbourhood no doubt hired by our opponents . . . It is expected 20 000 persons will be as spectators at the election from the neighbourhood, and they not only threaten to block up the road to prevent the candidates coming into the hall, but murder the freemen that vote for Roman Catholics, it being circulated by wicked persons in the neighbourhood that our candidates are Roman Catholics . . . The freemen cannot now walk the streets (even in day time) without insult. My windows have been broken, and unless some military horse are ordered from Mansfield or Lincoln lives will be lost.

Letter from John Parker to Lord Fitzwilliam, 23 May 1826

## Fear of change

Throughout the wars with France (1793-1815), the British Government had been afraid that the ideas behind the French Revolution would spread to Britain. It was thought that people who suggested any change or reform threatened revolution and the breakdown of society (source 12).

The Government continued to believe this even after the end of the war. A trade depression and unemployment caused much unrest, but the group most feared by the Government was the growing band of men who wanted political reform—the Radicals as they became known. The Radicals did not see themselves as particularly dangerous (source 13), but the Government's view was that reformers should be repressed. They started by attempting to prove that revolution was imminent (source 14). Later, it became known that such 'evidence' was obtained by spies who infiltrated political meetings; these men encouraged other people at the meeting to make rash and unlawful statements and then informed on them to the magistrates (source 15).

Not everyone believed that there was a danger of uprisings. Earl Fitzwilliam, for example, the Lord Lieutenant of the West Riding of Yorkshire reported to the Government that his area was quiet. However, there were riots in some parts of the country and the Government acted to crush this unrest (sources 16, 17).

In 1817 it suspended the people's right of habeas corpus—no imprisonment without trial. In the same year it passed the Seditious Meetings Act. This banned public meetings of more than fifty people unless seven householders signed a public announcement in a newspaper beforehand.

However, public meetings did continue. At one of these meetings on 16 August 1819, the Government's attitude to reform was finally made very clear.

### SOURCE 12

BELOW: This contemporary cartoon saw radical reform as a threat to life and liberty. Only loyalty (the lion) could save the country, depicted here as Britannia

DEATH or LIBERTY! or Britannia & the Virtues of the Constitution in danger of Violation from the great Political Libertine, Radical Reform

Around 50 000 people gathered at St Peter's Fields, Manchester. The local magistrates decided to use the military to arrest the main speaker, the Radical, Henry Hunt. In the rioting which followed eleven people were killed and over 400 wounded —many of them women. The event came to be known as the Peterloo Massacre (sources 18, 19).

The national sense of deep shock resulting from the Peterloo Massacre did not cause the Government to change its views. In fact even more severe steps were taken. Later in 1819 the Six Acts were passed. Among other measures, these Acts curbed the press, and made it even harder to hold meetings.

As the economic situation improved a little, agitation for political reform grew weaker. By 1820 it looked for the moment as though the Government's repressive measures had brought success.

BELOW LEFT: The massacre at Peterloo. The officer is saying, 'Cut them down, don't be afraid, they are not armed'

BELOW RIGHT: William Wentworth Fitzwilliam, Earl Fitzwilliam

ABOVE: One view of freedom of speech taken from a contemporary cartoon

### SOURCE 13 How Radicals saw themselves

The True Radical . . . thinks that government the best which meddles least and takes ןeast from the pockets of the people . . . He advocates democracy only because it seems most likely to prefer a system of this kind . . . He is for universal suffrage, annual parliaments, and vote by ballot, and thinks Whigs and Tories equally worthless as politicians. Though accused of violent inclinations . . . and called a savage and a firebrand, he is full of the milk of human kindness, and would not in the greatest rage hang more than a dozen loanmongers, or set fire to anything unless perhaps the stock Exchange, the Poor Law Bastilles, or the Bank.

*Northern Liberator*, 28 April 1838

### SOURCE 14 The Government view of the reformers' aims

It appears to your Committee . . . that attempts have been made, in various parts of the country to take advantage of the distress in which the labouring and manufacturing classes of the community are at present involved, to induce them to look for immediate relief, not only in a reform of Parliament but in a total overthrow of all existing establishments, and in a division of the landed property of the country.

Report of the Secret Committee of the House of Commons on the disturbed state of the country, 19 February 1817. *Parliamentary Debates*, XXXV, p. 441

### SOURCE 15 Encouragement from spies

From what I saw of Mr Cleary I was determined to watch his proceedings very narrowly . . . When I went to Manchester I made enquiry and it was with no small surprise that I learnt that EVERY MAN who had attended these [political] meetings had warrants issued against them except the said Mr Cleary. I found that these delegates, seven in number, had attended the Cock in Grafton Street by the appointment of Mr Cleary. That when they got there Mr Cleary led the conversation, and in the words of Mr Mitchell . . . he said, 'It was madness or folly for the leaders among the people to think of anything but physical force'.

Henry Hunt, *The Green Bag Plot*, 1819, pp. 13-14

## SOURCE 16 Lord Fitzwilliam gives a different view of unrest

I collect that the spirit of resistance to legitimate government is not spread wide even in these districts [Sheffield and Huddersfield]: on the contrary, that the number of revolutionists is very limited and confined, and that the mass of the people is still sound and well affected to the present [state] of things, and that everything above the very lowest orders feel and understand that their interests are at stake, and that they must be themselves active in preventing the success of the attempts they have witnessed.

Letter from Lord Fitzwilliam to Lord Sidmouth, 17 June 1817

## SOURCE 17 The Government deals with rioters, 1817

At the special commission held at Lancaster for the trial of the rioters of that period, eight persons were capitally convicted. At Chester, though fifteen were condemned to death, two only were ultimately executed. But the conduct pursued at Lancaster formed a striking contrast . . . There every person convicted, man, woman and child, were consigned to the hands of the executioner, one of these victims was a boy so young and childish, that he called on his mother for help at the time of his execution, thinking she had the power to save him.

Archibald Prentice, *Historical Sketches and Personal Recollections of Manchester*, London, 1851, pp. 56–7

## SOURCE 18 The procession to St Peter's Fields

From the windows of Mr Baxter's house . . . I saw the main body proceeding towards St Peter's Fields, and never saw a gayer spectacle . . . The 'marching order', of which so much was said afterwards, was what we often see now in the processions of Sunday-school children . . . Our company laughed at the fears of the magistrates, and the remark was, that if the men intended mischief they would not have brought their wives, their sisters, or their children with them.

Prentice, *Historical Sketches and Personal Recollections*, p. 159

## SOURCE 19 The Peterloo Massacre

In ten minutes from the commencement of the havock, the field was an open and almost deserted place. The sun looked down through a sultry and motionless air . . .

Several mounds of human beings still remained where they had fallen, crushed down

ABOVE: Archibald Prentice, author of *Historical Sketches and Personal Recollections*

and smothered. Some of these still groaning, others with staring eyes, were gasping for breath, and others would never breathe more. All was silent save these low sounds, and the occasional snorting and pawing of steeds.

Bamford, *Passages in the Life of a Radical*, Vol. I, pp. 206–8

ABOVE: Thomas Attwood, organiser of the Birmingham Political Union and an MP for Birmingham from 1832. The BPU was seen as respectable and non-violent, and formed the model for middle class organisations in other cities. Attwood became closely involved with the Chartists, and in July 1839 presented the 'monster petition' to the House of Commons

### SOURCE 20 One reason for avoiding reform

BELOW: St Stephens (Parliament) churns out money to be taken by parliamentary office holders. As one of them says, 'We are indebted to this system for all the blessings we enjoy'

## The Reform Act, 1832

We have seen that there were many reasons why Parliament should have been reformed. However, opposition to reform was strong. Many people did well out of the unreformed system, and some people honestly believed that the system should not be changed (sources 20-22). Others believed the time was not right (source 23)

Yet by 1830 it was becoming increasingly difficult to resist the need for change, particularly once the interest of the middle class was aroused. Their involvement brought organisation to the movement.

The strongest opponents of reform were the Tories under the leadership of the Duke of Wellington. They were supported by the King, George IV (sources 24, 25). However, George IV died in 1830, and was succeeded by his brother William IV. Soon afterwards, the Whigs, under Lord Grey, came to power; they were committed to parliamentary reform. Although Grey's Cabinet was dominated by aristocrats, it prepared a Bill to redistribute parliamentary seats from the rotten and pocket boroughs to the growing industrial towns. The franchise was also to be extended to include the middle classes.

Passing the Bill through Parliament proved difficult. At the first attempt it was thrown out by the Commons. At the second attempt, in October 1831, it was rejected by the Lords. Riots broke out throughout the country (source 26).

The Bill passed the Commons again in December, but again it was rejected by the Lords. Only when the King agreed to create fifty Whig peers did the Tory lords back down and the Bill was passed on 7 June 1832, without the need for new peers.

The Act did two things. First it increased the number of people who were allowed to vote. In the boroughs men owning or occupying property worth £10 a year or more were enfranchised, and in the counties a complicated set of conditions resulted in the vote being given to men who rented property as well as those who owned it. Even so, the total number of people allowed to vote was still only around 700 000 at the most; and this was in a population of about sixteen million. The second thing the Act did was to alter the distribution of parliamentary seats (sources 27, 28). Many large towns in England and Wales now gained two MPs each, and some smaller ones gained one each. Scotland was allocated eight new seats and Ireland five.

BELOW: The Reform Riots in Bristol, October 1831

Although the Reform Act was important, there were still many people who had no right to vote. And so the struggle continued.

### SOURCE 21 Why change a good system?

All the Anti-Reformers agreed in this, that . . . the present system had proved itself to be the best which ever had stood the test of experience, and as the nation had attained, and was enjoying under it, the highest degree of glory, prosperity, wealth and liberty, which it had ever possessed, the correction of minor abuses . . . ought to be gradually and cautiously attempted.

*Quarterly Review*, Murray, Vol. XLVI, 1832, p. 304

### SOURCE 22 The loss of good Members

If the boroughs of Knaresborough, of Tavistock, of Horsham, of Winchelsea, of Peterborough, were disfranchised, and the right of election were transferred to more populous places—to Birmingham, to Manchester, to Sheffield, to Leeds . . . I should regret very much [that] the House should be deprived of so many great lights.

Speech of George Canning, in *Quarterly Review*, Vol. XXII, 1820, p. 527

### SOURCE 23 Reform should be delayed

1. In a country like England, where the Government has been for ages based upon unjust distinctions . . . no very sweeping measure of Reform can be carried at the outset. Gradual changes are the only ones that can possibly be effected.
2. . . . the majority of the population are at present opposed to any further change.
3. That however just the claims of the lower class are, they have not the power, at present, to obtain them.

Extract from a letter by William Carpenter to *The Poor Man's Guardian*, 3 December 1831

### SOURCE 24 The case of the middle class

That honourable house [the Commons], in its present state, is . . . too far removed in habits, wealth and station, from the wants and interests of the lower and middle classes of the people . . . The great aristocratical interests are well represented there . . . But the interests of Industry and of Trade have scarcely any representatives at all! These, the most vital interests of the nation, the source of all its wealth and of all its strength, are comparatively unrepresented.

The Declaration of the Birmingham Political Union, 1830, p. 7

### SOURCE 25 George IV's attitude to reform

**8 August 1827**

The king recommends the cabinet to reorganise the government—

There was a distinct understanding between the king and his late lamented Minister [Mr Canning] (who had died) on many very important points.

The king will begin for example, by mentioning the question of parliamentary reform. The king joined with Mr Canning in giving his decided negative to that destructive project.

A. Aspinall (ed), *Letters of George IV*, Oxford University Press, 1938, p. 275

### SOURCE 26 Riots in Bristol, 1831

The whole of Bristol was on the verge of destruction; the mansion-house, custom-house, excise-office, and bishop's palace were plundered and set on fire; the toll gates pulled down, the prisons burst open with sledge hammers, and their inmates set at liberty . . . During the whole of the Sunday the mob were the unresisted masters of the city. Forty-two offices, dwelling-houses, and warehouses, were completely destroyed . . . The loss of property was estimated at half a million. The number of rioters killed, wounded or otherwise injured, were 110. Of about 14 or 16 who lost their lives, three died from the shots or sword-cuts of the military; the rest were mostly the victims of excessive drinking in the rifled cellars and warehouses, which produced either apoplexy upon the spot, or disabled them from escaping from the flames that they had themselves kindled.

Prentice, *Historical Sketches and Personal Recollections*, p. 401

ABOVE: George IV

**before 1832**

● Boroughs with under 50 voters
■ Boroughs with 50 – 499 voters

Each county returned at least one MP

| | | |
|---|---|---|
| 1. St. Ives | 50. Shaftesbury | 99. Banbury |
| 2. Helston | 51. Hindon | 100. Woodstock |
| 3. Penryn | 52. Downton | 101. Droitwich |
| 4. Truro | 53. Wilton | 102. Weobley |
| 5. St. Mawes | 54. Salisbury | 103. Brecon |
| 6. Grampound | 55. Old Sarum | 104. Haverfordwest |
| 7. Tregoney | 56. Heytesbury | 105. Bewdley |
| 8. Fowey | 57. Westbury | 106. Shrewsbury |
| 9. Lostwithiel | 58. Devizes | 107. Bishop's Castle |
| 10. Bodmin | 59. Calne | 108. Montgomery |
| 11. St. Michael | 60. Chippenham | 109. Wenlock |
| 12. Camelford | 61. Malmesbury | 110. Stafford |
| 13. Bossiney | 62. Wootton Bassett | 111. Tamworth |
| 14. Newport | 63. Marlborough | 112. Higham Ferrers |
| 15. Launceston | 64. Bedwyn | 113. Huntingdon |
| 16. Callington | 65. Ludgershall | 114. Cambridge & U. |
| 17. Liskeard | 66. Andover | 115. Maldon |
| 18. W. Looe | 67. Whitchurch | 116. Harwich |
| 19. E. Looe | 68. Stockbridge | 117. Bury St. Edmunds |
| 20. St. Germans | 69. Winchester | 118. Orford |
| 21. Saltash | 70. Petersfield | 119. Aldeburgh |
| 22. Plymouth | 71. Midhurst | 120. Dunwich |
| 23. Plympton | 72. Bramber | 121. Eye |
| 24. Beer Alston | 73. Arundel | 122. Thetford |
| 25. Tavistock | 74. Steyning | 123. King's Lynn |
| 26. Dartmouth | 75. Horsham | 124. Castle Rising |
| 27. Totnes | 76. E. Grinstead | 125. Boston |
| 28. Ashburton | 77. Lewes | 126. Grantham |
| 29. Okehampton | 78. Seaford | 127. E. Retford |
| 30. Barnstaple | 79. Hastings | 128. Beaumaris |
| 31. Tiverton | 80. Winchelsea | 129. Wigan |
| 32. Honiton | 81. Rye | 130. Newton |
| 33. Minehead | 82. New Romney | 131. Clitheroe |
| 34. Bridgwater | 83. Hythe | 132. Grimsby |
| 35. Taunton | 84. Sandwich | 133. Hedon |
| 36. Ilchester | 85. Queenborough | 134. Pontefract |
| 37. Milborne Port | 86. Bletchingley | 135. Malton |
| 38. Bath | 87. Reigate | 136. Knaresborough |
| 39. Lyme Regis | 88. Gatton | 137. Aldborough |
| 40. Melcombe Regis & Weymouth | 89. Haslemere | 138. Boroughbridge |
| | 90. Guildford | 139. Ripon |
| 41. Dorchester | 91. Windsor | 140. Thirsk |
| 42. Wareham | 92. Marlow | 141. Scarborough |
| 43. Corfe Castle | 93. Wycombe | 142. Northallerton |
| 44. Poole | 94. Agmondesham | 143. Richmond |
| 45. Christchurch | 95. Wendover | 144. Appleby |
| 46. Lymington | 96. Wallingford | 145. Cockermouth |
| 47. Yarmouth | 97. Buckingham | 146. Morpeth |
| 48. Newtown | 98. Brackley | |
| 49. Newport | | |

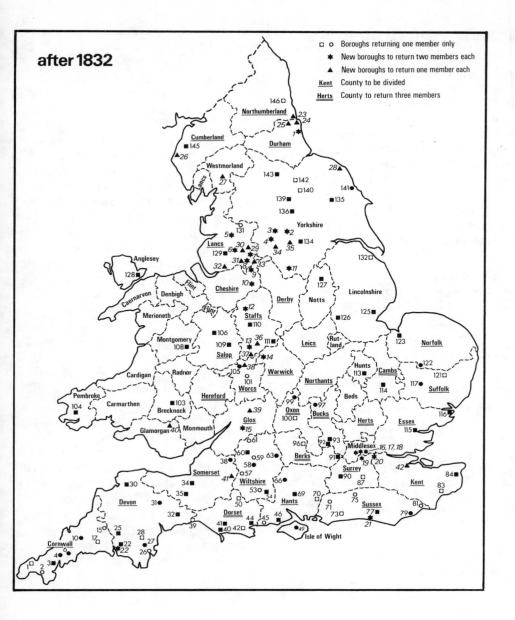

**after 1832**

□ ○ Boroughs returning one member only

★ New boroughs to return two members each

▲ New boroughs to return one member each

**Kent** County to be divided

**Herts** County to return three members

## SOURCE 28 Changes in parliamentary representation: The Reform Act, 7 June 1832

**Schedule A** [56 boroughs ceasing to return members]

Amersham, Wendover, Bossiney, Callington, Camelford, East Looe, Fowey, Lostwithiel, Newport, St Germans, St Mawes, St Michael (Midshall), Saltash, Tregony, West Looe, Beeralston, Okehampton, Plympton, Corfe Castle, Stockbridge, Whitchurch, Newtown, Yarmouth, Weobly, Queensborough, New Romney, Newton, Castle Rising, Higham Ferrers, Brackley, Bishop's Castle, Ilchester, Milborne Port, Minehead, Aldeburgh, Dunwich, Orford, Blechingley, Gatton, Haslemere, Bramber, East Grinstead, Seaford, Steyning, Winchelsea, Appleby, Great Bedwin, Downton, Heytesbury, Hindon, Ludgershall, Old Sarum, Wootton Bassett, Aldborough, Boroughbridge, Hedon.

**Schedule B** [30 boroughs to return one member only]

Wallingford, Helston, Launceston, Liskeard, St Ives, Ashburton, Dartmouth, Lyme Regis, Shaftesbury, Wareham, Christchurch, Peterfield, Hythe, Clitheroe, Great Grimsby, Morpeth, Woodstock, Eye, Reigate, Arundel, Horsham, Midhurst, Rye, Calne, Malmesbury, Westbury, Wilton, Droitwich, Northallerton, Thirsk.

A. Aspinall and E. A. Smith (ed), *English Historical Documents 1783–1832*, Eyre and Spottiswoode, 1959, pp. 352–3

*To return two members each*

| | | |
|---|---|---|
| 1. Sunderland | 19. Lambeth | 35. Wakefield |
| 2. Leeds | 20. Greenwich | 36. Walsall |
| 3. Bradford | 21. Brighton | 37. Dudley |
| 4. Halifax | 22. Devonport | 38. Kidderminster |
| 5. Blackburn | | 39. Cheltenham |
| 6. Bolton | *To return one member each* | 40. Merthyr Tydfil |
| 7. Oldham | 23. Tynemouth | 41. Frome |
| 8. Manchester | 24. South Shields | 42. Chatham |
| 9. Stockport | 25. Gateshead | |
| 10. Macclesfield | 26. Whitehaven | |
| 11. Sheffield | 27. Kendal | |
| 12. Stoke-on-Trent | 28. Whitby | |
| 13. Wolverhampton | 29. Rochdale | |
| 14. Birmingham | 30. Bury | |
| 15. Stroud | 31. Salford | |
| 16. Marylebone | 32. Warrington | |
| 17. Finsbury | 33. Ashton-under-Lyne | |
| 18. Tower Hamlets | 34. Huddersfield | |

## Chartism: the first years

Many working men felt that the 1832 Reform Act had brought them no benefit; some had predicted this even before the Bill was passed (source 29).

Some of the abuses of the old system remained, so there was still room for a movement which would extend the right to vote to all classes of society. This movement became known as Chartism. In the North it was closely linked with the struggle against the New Poor Law and with the agitation for factory reform. Its first objective was constitutional change, but it grew out of social and economic distress.

In 1836, the London Working Men's Association was formed with William Lovett as leader. The Charter it produced in 1838 aimed at improving the social and economic situation by having working class Members of Parliament who would represent their own class interests.

The movement found one of its leaders in Feargus O'Connor. He had bought a newspaper, *The Northern Star*, in 1837 which he was using to support the working class cause.

The main problem faced by the Chartists was how to get the Government to take notice of the six points. Some believed in 'moral force'—putting up a good case in the form of a National Petition (sources 30-32). Yet working class bitterness at continued exclusion from political power encouraged other beliefs, and at large meetings like the one held in 1838 on Pepe Green, there were demands for violence (source 33).

When Parliament rejected the Chartist Petition in 1839 a general uprising was planned. In the event though, there was only one attempt at violence. The Chartist leader John Frost led 4000 miners against the town of Newport. However, the uprising was badly led, troops were used against the miners, and Frost was transported to Tasmania (source 34).

By 1840 most of the Chartist leaders, including O'Connor, were in prison.

BELOW: This page from a Chartist newspaper questions the Reform Act

### THE LYING WHIG REFORM BILL;

THE FOLLOWING TABLES EXHIBIT THE MONSTROUS DELUSION THAT THE REFORM BILL DESTROYED THE ROTTEN BOROUGH SYSTEM.

**1.—Contested Elections, 1837, and subsequently, at which the votes polled for a successful candidate were less than 200.**

| | BOROUGH OR COUNTY. | RETURNS | POLLED | CONSTITUENCY FROM WHOM FORMED. | POPULATION. |
|---|---|---|---|---|---|
| 1 | Ashburton | 1 | 98 | 101 nom. freem.&342 h. | 4,165 |
| 2 | Arundel | 1 | 176 | 380 £10 h. | 2,803 |
| 3 | Banbury | 1 | 185 | old cor. of 18 & 365 h. | 5,906 |
| 4 | Bandon (Ireland) | 1 | 133 | 13 f. and 279 h. | 9,820 |
| 5 | Brecon | 1 | 151 | 350 h. | 5,026 |
| 6 | Caithnesshire | 1 | 198 | | 34,000 |
| 7 | Carlow (Ireland) | 1 | 167 | 23 f. and 403 h. | 9,012 |
| 8 | Cockermouth | 2 | 117 | burghage holders&235h. | 6,022 |
| 9 | Colerain (Ireland) | 1 | 129 | 52 f. and 240 h. | 5,752 |
| 10 | Devizes | 2 | 109 | cor. and 409 h. | 6,367 |
| 11 | Downpatrick (I.) | 1 | 190 | | 4,779 |
| 12 | Eversham | 2 | 168 | 130 h. | 3,991 |
| 13 | Frome | 1 | 125 | 450 h. | 12,240 |
| 14 | Harwich | 1 | 75 | cor. and 202 h. | 4,297 |
| 15 | Helston | 1 | 160 | cor. and 225 h. | 3,293 |
| 16 | Horsham | 1 | 147 | burghage tenants & 365h | 5,105 |
| 17 | Kidderminster | 1 | 198 | 500 h. | 20,165 |
| 18 | Kinsale (Ireland) | 1 | 102 | 301 h. | 6,897 |
| 19 | Knaresborough | 2 | 172 | burghage tenants&369h | 6,252 |
| 20 | Liskeard | 1 | 113 | cor. and 315 h. | 4,042 |
| 21 | Ludlow | 2 | 194 | b. and 314 h. | 5,252 |
| 22 | Lyme Regis | 1 | 121 | f. and 300 h. | 3,345 |
| 23 | Lymington | 2 | 161 | cor. and 189 h. | 5,472 |
| 24 | Petersfield | 1 | 125 | freeh. and 305 h. | 4,922 |
| 25 | Sligo (Ireland) | 1 | 178 | 13 f. and 680 h. | 12,762 |
| 26 | Totness | 2 | 158 | f. and 316 h. | 9,562 |
| 27 | Tralee (Ireland) | 1 | 75 | 13 f. and 354 h. | 3,442 |
| 28 | Wallingford | 1 | 159 | cor. and 278 h. | 2,467 |
| 29 | Wareham | 1 | 170 | s. and c. and 54 h. | 2,566 |
| 30 | Woodstock | 1 | 126 | f. and 373 h. | 7,055 |
| 31 | Youghal (Ireland) | 1 | 158 | f. and 479 h. | 9,600 |

**2.—Contested Elections, and voters polled under 300.**

| | BOROUGH OR COUNTY | RETURNS | POLLED | CONSTITUENCY FROM WHOM FORMED | POPULATION. |
|---|---|---|---|---|---|
| 1 | Armagh (Ireland) | 1 | 235 | 13 f. and 520 h. | 9,189 |
| 2 | Ashton-under-Lyne | 1 | 234 | 610 h. | 14,673 |
| 3 | Banffshire | 1 | 292 | | 48,000 |
| 4 | Bodmin | 1 | 200 | c. and 311 h. | 5,228 |
| 5 | Bridport | 2 | 283 | s. and l., and 342 h. | 4,242 |
| 6 | Buckingham | 2 | 235 | c. and 225 h. | 3,610 |
| 7 | Bury | 1 | 248 | 765 h. | 15,086 |
| 8 | Bury St. Edmunds | 2 | 289 | 719 | 11,436 |
| 9 | Clonmell (Ireland) | 1 | 284 | 94 f. and 752 h. | 12,256 |
| 10 | Gateshead | 1 | 266 | 750 h. | 15,177 |
| 11 | Guildford | 2 | 252 | f. and 431 h. | 3,916 |
| 12 | Haddingshire | 1 | 299 | | 36,100 |
| 13 | Ditto Districts | 1 | 268 | 214 h. | |
| 14 | Haverfordwest do. | 1 | 247 | s. and l., and 584 h. | 10,832 |
| 15 | Honiton | 2 | 294 | s. and l., and 318 h. | 3,509 |
| 16 | Hythe | 1 | 243 | f. and 537 h. | 6,903 |
| 17 | Inverness-shire | 1 | 254 | | 94,800 |
| 18 | Kirkaldy Burghs | 1 | 216 | | |
| 19 | Londonderry (I.) | 1 | 214 | f. and 735 h. | 14,020 |
| 20 | Newport (I. of W.) | 2 | 264 | f. and 445 h. | 6,796 |
| 21 | Peebleshire | 1 | 251 | | 10,600 |
| 22 | Poole | 2 | 272 | f. and 298 h. | 6,959 |
| 23 | Scarborough | 2 | 225 | c. and 508 h. | 8,760 |
| 24 | Selkirkshire | 1 | 230 | | 6,800 |
| 25 | Shaftesbury | 1 | 221 | s. and l., and 145 h. | 8,518 |
| 26 | St. Albans | 2 | 252 | s. and l., and 286 h. | 5,771 |
| 27 | St. Andrews | 1 | 290 | 452 h. | |
| 28 | Tewkesbury | 2 | 219 | f. and 262 h. | 5,780 |
| 29 | Teignmouth | 1 | 259 | 1,150 h. | 23,206 |
| 30 | Warrington | 1 | 278 | 973 h. | 18,184 |
| 31 | Weymouth | 2 | 289 | c. and 490 h. | 8,095 |
| 32 | Wigan | 2 | 268 | b. and 568 h. | 20,774 |
| 33 | Winchester | 2 | 259 | b. and 807 h. | 9,212 |

NOTE.—C., corporation; s. and l. scot and lot voters; f., freeman; h., occupants of houses at an annual rental of £10 and upwards.

## SOURCE 29 Working men and the Reform Act

. . . Meetings are everywhere holden but by whom are these meetings convened and by whom attended? . . . Why, by your hypocritical time-serving property-loving 'middlemen' . . . Yes, friends and fellow-countrymen, we protest that this measure is a mere trick. It is clear, we GAIN nothing by it; but it is said, that these middlemen will be more inclined to hear our appeal for justice, and will return a majority favourable to it; think it not . . . do they not plainly tell you, that they like not universal suffrage?

*The Poor Man's Guardian*, 24 September 1831

## SOURCE 30 The Charter

### The six points of the People's Charter

1. A vote for every man twenty one years of age, of sound mind, and not undergoing punishment for crime.

2. THE BALLOT—To protect the elector in the exercise of his vote.

3. NO PROPERTY QUALIFICATION for Members of Parliament—thus enabling the constituencies to return the man of their choice, be he rich or poor.

4. PAYMENT OF MEMBERS, thus enabling an honest tradesman, working man, or other person, to serve a constituency, when taken from his business to attend to the interests of the country.

5. EQUAL CONSTITUENCIES, securing the same amount of representation for the same number of electors,—instead of allowing small constituencies to swamp the votes of larger ones.

6. ANNUAL PARLIAMENTS, thus presenting the most effectual check to bribery and intimidation, since though a constituency might be bought once in seven years (even with the ballot), no purse could buy a constituency (under a system of universal suffrage) in each ensuing twelvemonth; and since members, when elected for a year only, would not be able to defy and betray their constituents as now.

A handbill quoted in G. D. H. Cole & A. W. Filson, *British Working Class Movements*, Macmillan, 1967, p. 352

### SOURCE 31 Feargus O'Connor

No member of the prize ring could fight his way with more desperate energy through a crowd than could this electioneering pugilist; and it was not alone with his fists that he was useful to his friends. A barrister by profession . . . he could plead the cause of a candidate on the hustings with no little share of persuasive power.

R. G. Gammage, *History of the Chartist Movement,* Newcastle-upon-Tyne, 1894, p. 14

### SOURCE 32 The first National Petition

It was the fond expectation of the people that a remedy for the greater part of their grievances, would be found in the Reform Act of 1832 . . . They have been bitterly and basely deceived . . .

The Reform Act has effected a transfer of power from one domineering faction to another, and left the people as helpless as before . . . When the State calls for defenders, when it calls for money, no consideration of poverty or ignorance can be pleaded, in refusal or delay of the call. We perform the duties of freemen; we must have the privileges for freemen. Therefore, we demand universal suffrage. The suffrage, to be exempt from the corruption of the wealthy and the violence of the powerful, must be **secret.**

From the National Petition; in Cole & Filson, *British Working Class Movements,* pp. 354-5

### SOURCE 33 O'Connor and violence

So the magistrates think of putting down our meeting by acts of violence? . . . I am quite ready . . . to stand by the law, and not give our tyrants the slightest advantage in attacking us in sections; but should they employ force against us, I am for repelling attack with attack.

O'Connor's speech at Pepe Green; quoted in Gammage, *History of the Chartist Movement,* p. 113

ABOVE: Feargus O'Connor. Unlike Lovett, O'Connor was willing to use violence to achieve success for the Chartists

ABOVE: An artist's view of the Chartist riots at Newport in 1839. It makes an interesting comparison with Gammage's account of what happened (source 34)

## SOURCE 34 The Newport attack

A company of the 45th Regiment was stationed at the Westgate Hotel, and thither the multitude marched, loudly cheering as they proceeded through the streets. Arrived in front of the Hotel, an attack was immediately commenced; the magistrates, police, and specials were driven from the streets, and fled into the Hotel for refuge. The soldiers were stationed at the windows, through which a number of the people began to fire . . . The soldiers, as a matter of course, returned the fire . . . the consequence was, that in about twenty minutes ten of the Chartists were killed upon the spot, and about fifty others wounded.

Gammage, *History of the Chartist Movement*, p. 162

# Chartism: 1840–48

In July 1840, at a conference in Manchester, Chartist delegates supporting O'Connor decided to reorganise the Chartist movement into the National Charter Association. They decided to present another petition.

Now competing with the Anti-Corn Law League for working class support, the Chartists managed to collect over three million signatures. The petition reached the House of Commons early in 1842. It was rejected in April. This time, working class reaction took the form of strikes in the factory areas. Magistrates' houses were attacked, and factories disrupted or destroyed. The technique of knocking out the steam boiler plugs at chosen factories and thus destroying their power source, earned the strikes the name 'The Plug Plot' (sources 35, 36).

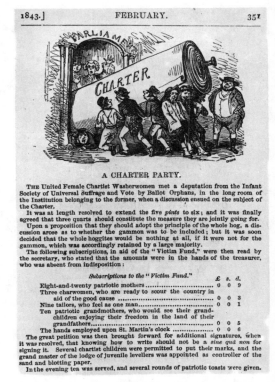

ABOVE: Not everyone took the Chartists seriously

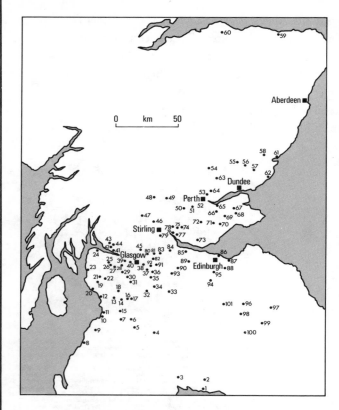

## Chartist Groups in Scotland

Chartism in Scotland took a more moderate form than in Wales or northern England. The organisers were lower middle rather than working class, and believed that better education and self help would achieve their aims, not violent action

**Chartist Associations in Scotland**

1. Annan
2. Ecclefechan
3. Dumfries
4. Sanquhar
5. New Cumnock
6. Cumnock
7. Ochiltree and Sorn
8. Girvan
9. Maybole
10. Ayr
11. Prestwick
12. Irvine
13. Kilmarnock
14. Galston
15. Mauchline
16. Newmilns
17. Darvel
18. Fenwick
19. Dalry
20. Saltcoats
21. Kilbirnie
22. Beith
23. Largs
24. Greenock
25. Bridge of Weir
26. Kilbarchan
27. Johnstone
28. Paisley
29. Barrhead
30. Newtonmearns
31. Eaglesham
32. Strathaven
33. Lanark
34. Stonehouse
35. Hamilton
36. Bellshill
37. Uddingston
38. Shettleston
39. Govan
40. Renfrew
41. Dumbarton
42. Vale of Leven
43. Alexandria
44. Bonhill
45. Balfron
46. Doune
47. Callander
48. Comrie
49. Crieff
50. Auchterarder
51. Dunning
52. Crossgates
53. Bridgend
54. Blairgowrie
55. Kirriemuir
56. Forfar
57. Letham
58. Brechin
59. Banff
60. Elgin
61. Montrose
62. Arbroath
63. Cupar-Angus
64. New Scone
65. Newburgh
66. Auchtermuchty
67. Cupar
68. Ceres
69. Kettle
70. Markinch
71. Leslie
72. Kinross
73. Dunfermline
74. Dollar
75. Tillicoultry
76. Alva
77. Clackmannan
78. Alloa
79. Bannockburn
80. Lennoxtown
81. Milton
82. Kirkintilloch
83. Kilsyth
84. Falkirk
85. Linlithgow
86. Leith
87. Musselburgh
88. Dalkeith
89. Bathgate
90. Whitburn
91. Airdrie
92. Coatbridge
93. Shotts
94. West Linton
95. Penicuik
96. Galashiels
97. Kelso
98. Selkirk
99. Jedburgh
100. Hawick
101. Innerleithen

*Note:* within the major towns— Glasgow, Edinburgh, Dundee and Aberdeen— there were numerous local associations

Once again, troops were used and local volunteer forces were raised. The strikers were imprisoned or transported.

The movement seemed beaten. The general economic situation improved after 1842, and O'Connor put most of his effort into the Chartist Land Scheme—an attempt to settle workers on the land as peasant proprietors.

However, the financial collapse of the National Land Company in 1847 turned the Chartists back to their political demands. They set to work to organise their third petition.

Meetings were held all over the country, and a National Assembly was planned for London in April 1848, to be followed by a mass procession to present the petition to Parliament.

The year 1848 was a year of revolutions in Europe. So the Government, fearing an uprising by the Chartists, took elaborate precautions. The fiasco of the Chartist meeting on Kennington Common on 10 April finally showed the weakness of the agitation. The police prevented the procession from taking place, and the petition had to be delivered by horse-cab travelling through back streets. Then it was discovered that there were fewer signatures than had been claimed and many were forgeries (sources 37-39).

The influence of Chartism as a national movement had been destroyed. Opponents' attitudes changed from fear to ridicule.

Yet in this survey we have only looked at part of the story. It would be interesting to consider, for example, how many of the Chartists' six points we accept today.

ABOVE: Thomas Cooper
ABOVE RIGHT: The Chartists' meeting on Kennington Common, London, 10 April 1848. Although the demonstration was a failure, the meeting itself was peaceful, despite earlier predictions of trouble

## SOURCE 35 Rallying Chartist support

. . . When we get the Charter we will repeal the Corn Laws and all other bad laws. But if you give up your agitation for the Charter to help the Free Traders, they will not help you to get the Charter. Don't be deceived by the middle classes again. You helped them to get their votes—you swelled their cry of 'The bill, the whole bill, and nothing but the bill!' But where are the fine promises you made? Gone to the winds! They said when they had gotten their votes, they would help you to get yours. But they and the rotten Whigs have never remembered you . . . And now they want to get the Corn Laws repealed—not for your benefit—but for their own. 'Cheap Bread!' they cry. But they mean 'Low Wages!' Do not listen to their cant and humbug. Stick to your Charter. You are slaves without your votes!

Thomas Cooper, *The Life, written by himself*, London, 1872, pp. 136–7

### SOURCE 36 The Plug Plot in Leeds

On the morning of the 17th (August, 1842) the greatest excitement prevailed in Leeds, from a report that a vast number of rioters were on the road from Bradford. The town of Leeds was well organised with troops, and a large number of special constables had been sworn in . . . Meantime a large mob had assembled at Hunslet, and commenced operations by turning out the hands at Messrs. Petty's potteries; after which they went along Holbeck Moor to the mills in Holbeck. They forced in the boiler plug and summoned the hands out of the mill of Messrs. E. and G. Tatham . . . They then proceeded to the mill of Messrs Titley, Tatham and Walker, Water Lane, which they were engaged in stopping when Prince George with the Lancers came up at full speed, and formed in line in Camp Field. The riot act was read, and two or three of the ring leaders were taken prisoners.

John Mayhall, *Annals of Leeds, York and the Surrounding District*, 1865, p. 143

### SOURCE 37 1848 in Europe

**25 March 1848**

Nothing is more extraordinary than to look back at my last date and see what has happened in the course of five days . . . within these last four or five days there has been a desperate battle in the streets of Berlin between the soldiers and the mob; the flight of the Prince of Prussia . . . Next a revolution in Austria; a riot in Vienna; downfall and flight of Metternich; riots in Milan; . . . Hungary up and doing and the whole empire in a state of dissolution. Throughout Germany all the people stirring; all the sovereigns yielding to the popular demands; the King of Hanover submitting to the terms demanded of him; the King of Bavaria abdicating.

L. Strachey and R. Fulford (eds), *The Greville Memoirs*, Macmillan, 1938, Vol. VI, pp. 158-9

### SOURCE 38 London prepares for the Chartists

*April 5:* The alarm about the Chartists increases. Everybody expects that the attack will be serious.

*April 9:* The alarm of to-day is very general all over the town . . . The Duke of Wellington is to command the troops, and the orders he has given are that the police are to go first to disperse the meeting; if resistance is offered and they are likely to be beaten, then the troops are instantly to appear, and the cannon to open with shell and grenades, infantry and cavalry are to charge—in short, they are to be made an example of.

Lord Malmesbury, *Memoirs of an Ex-Minister*, Longman, 1885, Vol. I, pp. 223-4

## SOURCE 39 The Chartist Petition of 1848

. . . The number of signatures has been ascertained to be 1 975 496. It is further evident to your Committee, that on numerous consecutive sheets the signatures are in one and the same handwriting. Your Committee also observed the names of distinguished individuals . . . who can scarcely be supposed to concur in its prayer: among which occurs the name of Her Majesty, as Victoria Rex, April 1st, F.M. Duke of Wellington, Sir Robert Peel, etc. etc. Your Committee have also observed . . . the insertion of numbers of names which are obviously fictitious, such as 'No Cheese', 'Pug Nose' 'Flat Nose'.

*Hansard*, 3/XCVIII/284-301

LEFT: The cartoonist George Cruickshank provides a popular view of what would happen to Parliament if the Chartists' demands were accepted

C

# The Sunderland By-Election

## Introduction

The result of the Sunderland by-election of 1841 surprised contemporaries. The favourite lost.

We shall see that the election was very controversial, but on the evidence, it may be that the election was decided not so much on the matters discussed, but on other issues.

LEFT: William Thompson

## The candidates

The 1832 Reform Act had given the port of Sunderland on the Durham coast the right to elect two MPs for Parliament.

From 1833 to 1841, one MP was a Whig (liberal) and the other a Tory. In September 1841, the Tory MP resigned. He was William Thompson, an alderman and ex-Lord Mayor of the City of London, and he resigned because he wanted to stand for election in the more important county seat of Westmorland. This seat had become vacant because one of the sitting members, Lord Lowther, had succeeded his father as Earl of Lonsdale and had moved to the House of Lords.

The Whig candidate for the resulting by-election in Sunderland was Viscount Howick, son of Earl Grey, sponsor of the Reform Bill. Howick had been defeated in the general election in the North Northumberland constituency, but wanted very much to return to Parliament despite the great expense of a contested election (source 40).

ABOVE: Viscount Howick—a cartoon from *Vanity Fair*
OPPOSITE: Sunderland in the 1840s

BELOW: Wolverley Attwood

**SOURCE 40 Howick describes in his Journal how he came to Sunderland to contest the election**

On Thursday Septr 9th I had been with George Grey . . . to see the works of the new harbour at the mouth of the Coquet & the lighthouse on the island & we only got back at ½ past 5 when I was told that 3 gentlemen from Sunderland were waiting in the library to speak to me. I went to them & found that they were Mr. Featherstonehaugh, Mr. Wm. Robinson, & Mr. Hutton Chaytor who came as a deputatn to ask me to become a candidate for the seat for Sunderland which Alderman Thompson had just vacated in order to come in for Westmoreland in the place of Ld Lowther called up to the Lds. They brought . . . a requisition to me to stand very hastily got up but still signed by a good many of the leaders of the liberal party in the town. Upon talking the subject over with them . . . the expense they assured me wd. not exceed 800 £. With this information I went to my father who was in his room resting as usual at that hour . . . He advised me to accept the invitatn & to set off as soon as possible, accordingly I returned to the library told the gentlemen who were there that I wd. stand as they wished & settled that they shd stay dinner & that immediately afterwards I shd. go back with them in the phaeton in which they had come . . . We did not get to Newcastle till near two in the morning & it was agreed that I shd. take a bed there & follow them to Sunderland by the 9 o'clock train. They went on to get the Commee assembled & preparations made for an immediate canvass. I got to Sunderland a little before 10 in the morning (Friday Septr 10th) & found a large party waiting for me at the inn & handbills printed announcing that I shd. address the electors ar 12 o'clock. After saying a few words to my friends who were in the room stating that my expenses must be confined to those strictly legal & necessary I started at once upon my canvass which proved exceedingly successful. At 12 I came back to the inn made a speech to the assembled crowd & then resumed my canvass which I continued without interruptn till ½ past six.
Viscount Howick, *Journal*, 9 September 1841

The Tory candidate was Matthias Wolverley Attwood. He was a prominent London banker, nephew of Thomas Attwood of the Birmingham Political Union and Chairman of The General Steam Navigation Company. He had recently failed to win a seat for London in the general election, but it was thought that his connection with shipping and his personal wealth would make him a strong candidate in Sunderland.

The third important political element in Sunderland was the Chartists who were particularly strong. Their leaders, George Binns and James Williams, played an important part in the by-election. They had hoped to put forward a candidate of their own, Colonel Perronet Thompson (Handbill 2), but he declined to stand, probably because Howick was already campaigning and he did not want to split the liberal vote.

## The issues

The campaign focused on both local and national issues.

### Sunderland's prosperity

Sunderland's importance as the centre of the coal trade had declined. This was partly because, as Howick pointed out, Lord Londonderry had built his own port of Seaham Harbour further down the coast (Handbill 3). However, in two speeches made on 10 and 11 September, Attwood questioned whether Howick and the Whigs were really the men to represent Sunderland's trading interests:

### SOURCE 41 Attwood poses as the champion of Sunderland's prosperity

Gentlemen, what are our views as distinguished from his [Howick's]? Ours are essentially commercial, and not only political . . . And is not my Lord Howick not only the representative of these political principles which we condemn, but also of those principles of commercial government which . . . produce destruction and ruin to our commerce? . . . We do not wish to see legislators dealing with important interests upon which they have no practical knowledge . . . We want them dealt with by practical men in a practical way . . .

. . . Gentlemen, I do not simply offer myself to you as a man professing certain political opinions, but I venture to present myself as connected with those commercial interests in which you have so deep a stake, and as being identified with those trading and shipping interests which predominate in Sunderland; and I do think that I may fairly, as a commercial candidate, offer myself for this commercial borough (loud applause)· There is indeed no place in this country which is under a greater necessity of sending to parliament men practically acquainted with its mercantile interests (applause). I know that Sunderland is largely connected with shipping, and I know that no men have more right to complain of ignorant and injurious legislation than the shipowners (loud applause).

Speeches by Wolverley Attwood, 10 and 11 September 1841

### The Corn Laws

Howick made it clear that he was opposed to the Corn Laws:

### SOURCE 42 Howick on the Corn Laws

. . . You know that the great line of distinction between opposing parties at this moment is respecting the financial and commercial policy recommended by the two great parties . . . On the one side you have a party insisting on . . . maintaining protection, and

## Lord Howick
### A
## WARMING
## PAN.

THE ELECTORS of Sunderland have now the most Crafty Trick played off upon them that has yet been attempted on any occasion, by the Lambton clique, to grasp the entire representation of the Borough. It is no less than to deprive the electors of their suffrages and to make them the degraded instruments of serving the factious political purposes of Lord Howick, after his rejection by the independent YEOMANRY of Northumberland. It is notorious that Lord Howick cares nothing for, and understands nothing of Commercial Interests, and that his only object is to get into Parliament for party and selfish purposes, to palm himself and kindred into place and power in the same disgraceful manner as has been witnessed in the course of the last ten years, when not a member of the numerous and Hungry Family of Grey were without a good place or a rich Pension. The whole family are now pensioners on the impoverished treasury of the Country, in return for scandalous jobbing, the reckless, ignorant and mischievous system of Government, which characterised the Grey Administration, and which has brought the Country to the verge of bankruptcy, and the working classes to pinching poverty. But despicable as has been the political conduct of Lord Howick, the presumption and trickery in putting him forward to represent Sunderland, is the most matchless effrontery that Sir Hedworth Williamson and the Lambton Faction have yet attempted. Lord Howick is only sent here as a Warming Pan to prepare the seat for some other Whig Adventurer, and if he were to be elected now, at the next Election, come when it may, the Borough of Sunderland will be handed over in the same way to some other tool of Sir Hedworth's and the Lambton Agents.

Lord Howick is pledged to contest the Northern Division of Northumberland, whenever a vacancy may happen, as may be proved by an extract from his speech on the Hustings at Alnwick, on the 19th of July last, when he was sent adrift by the Electors of Northumberland. On that memorable and glorious occasion, Lord Howick said "he trusted they, the Howick Party, would not slacken in their determination to recover what they had now lost; and if they honoured him with their confidence, at a suitable period he should again come forward, and to fight that battle, he would remind them to lose no time in making preparations for it." It is also well known in Northumberland that Lord Howick is privately pledged to his friends and party to contest that County, and therefore on this occasion he is only the Warming Pan of the Williamson and Lambton Party, and has no object to serve but his own personal ambition.

Electors of Sunderland,

## Reject the Warming Pan Howick!
### AND
## Elect Attwood
#### As your future and faithful Representative.

Sunderland, September 13, 1841.

**Sunderland: Printed by T. Hodge.**

ABOVE: Handbill 1. Howick a warming pan

# ELECTION

**The following resolutions were unanimously passed at the great PUBLIC MEETING, on Friday Evening, in the Arcade :---**

1st,--That this Meeting, having seen a bill issued by the Whigs, requesting the Electors to withhold their support from Lord Dungannon, hereby expresses its approval of the same, and calls upon the Electors to withhold their support from any man, whether representing Whigs or Tories.

2nd,---That this Meeting is determined to give the Tory Parliament a proof that the people of Sunderland are dissatisfied with the mis-rule of faction; and it pledges itself to hold no parley with men or parties who will not strike a blow at the despotism that grinds us to the dust.

3rd,--That this Meeting awaits the return of Mr. Williams from London, before they surrender their Suffrages to any man in the field, as they deem the great question of Parliamentary Reform so important, that the Candidate for our representation should be an out-and-out REFORMER.

4th,--That a Committee of Electors and Non-Electors be chosen by this Meeting, to commence immediately a vigorous canvas of the Borough, for a man who will reform the Representation of the Country on the Principles of the People's Charter, and advocate the removal of all those restrictions on trade which make food dear and labour scarce.

**Mr. WILLIAMS will address the People of Sunderland at the Life-Boat House, on Sunday afternoon, at half-past 2 o'Clock.**

# ELECTORS!!

Withhold your Votes till the Polling day, as

## Another Candidate will enter the field.

PRINTED BY J. WILLIAMS, BRIDGE-STREET, BISHOPWEARMOUTH.

---

TO THE

# ELECTORS
OF
# SUNDERLAND.

IF your object in choosing a Member be to PROMOTE, instead of DISCOURAGING, the Trade of your Port, you surely can have no difficulty in deciding between a Tory and a Reformer—between Mr. Attwood and Viscount Howick.

You have been told a great deal of a Repeal of Taxes.

Who repealed the Export Duty on Coals, by which the Export Trade of the North of England has been increased from 410,000 to 1,156,000 tons? Was it the Tories? Was it the Duke of Wellington or Sir Robert Peel, whom Mr. Attwood promises to support---of whose faction, indeed, he is the tool? No!

Wellington and Peel always resisted and refused the Repeal of the Coal Duty; but the Whig Government conceded it. And not only did the Tories refuse to take off the Coal Duty, but their newspaper organs in London have been abusing the Whigs for doing so, and giving significant hints of a Tory intention to lay on the Duty again.

Lord Londonderry built Seaham Harbour, and, by doing so, took away a large portion of your Trade. Are you desirous that the Tories should lay on the Coal Duty again, and thereby take away the remainder?

The Tories are knaves, and, in the very blindness of their rascality, they take you, the Electors of Sunderland, to be fools!!!

# HOWICK
AND
# THE TRADE OF SUNDERLAND
## FOR EVER!

. . . maintaining under that name, restrictions . . . upon almost every branch of our industry, above all restrictions upon the trade in the first article of human subsistence—I mean corn. On the other side you have those (and it is among these we have taken our stand) who are of the opinion that the commerce of this country can only be made to revive . . . by . . . a decided advance towards a more liberal commercial policy . . . Can any man doubt the stagnation of trade of which you have cause to complain . . . in this town . . . arises very much from the consequence of bad harvests, aggravated by the existing corn-law?

Speech by Viscount Howick, 10 September 1841

Attwood agreed that changes might be necessary, but he also gave a warning:

### SOURCE 43 Attwood on the Corn Laws

. . . I now have to say a few words on the great question of the corn laws—a question which is one of a commercial nature, and ought not to be confused with politics (hear, hear). I can assure you that I am as anxious for a beneficial alteration in those laws as any man can be (hear, hear). I do think some alteration in the corn laws desirable, and I am prepared to go into the question, and do everything in my power to render the price of bread as low as possible, that will not inflict injury in some

other way (loud applause). Gentlemen, but so far as the interests of the labouring classes are concerned, we must take care that in lowering the price of corn, we do not lower the wages of labour also. In these foreign countries in which corn is cheaply grown, wages are so low that the labourer never tastes wheaten bread (cheers).

Speech by Wolverley Attwood, 11 September 1841

### The Poor Law

The Poor Law Amendment Act (1834) was still a controversial topic. Wolverley Attwood claimed that when he had been an MP he had opposed the measures introduced by the Act:

### SOURCE 44 Attwood on the Poor Law

. . . Gentlemen, it is my pride and boast, that from the moment that measure was introduced, to soften its severity, my utmost exertions have been directed, during the time I have had the honour of a seat in parliament; because, though I have always considered it just to correct abuse in the administration of relief to the poor and to prevent the encouragement of idle and improvident paupers, yet that in order to provide against such abuses, it was unjust to adopt a system, harsh and oppressive to the honest and industrious pauper, whom it ought to be the object of such a law to provide for (applause); and against that I have ever raised my voice and

trust I ever shall do. (Applause.) And when we look to the spirit in which that measure has been dealt with by the Liberals, it has given us a test by which we may judge of what their sentiment to the poor really is.

. . . When I hear any public man calling himself a friend of the poor, I look to the part that man has taken in reference to the New Poor Law when it has been before the house (hear, hear). For my own part, I can assure you that there has been no more zealous opponent of its severe and unnecessarily restrictive clauses in the House of Commons than myself. That question, gentlemen, is one real practical test to which I can refer when I tell you that, if you do me the honour to elect me as your representative, I shall be the ardent and sincere friend, not only of the shipping and trading interests, but of the working classes (renewed cheering).

Speeches by Wolverley Attwood, 10 and 11 September 1841

FAR LEFT: Handbill 2. Another candidate will enter the field. At one time it was thought that Lord Dungannon would be the Tory candidate, but he withdrew in favour of Attwood
LEFT: Handbill 3. Howick and the trade of Sunderland for ever

RIGHT: Handbill 4.
£125 bribe

# £125 BRIBE!!

To conceal the proceedings of a Pick-pocket, or permit a Thimble-rigger to to practise his swindling arts upon his unfortunate dupes, would, by every man of common sense and honesty, be regarded as a gross breach of duty, and a virtual participation in those crimes. But what is the crime of a pick-pocket or a thimble-rigger, to that of the man, or the party, that would buy and sell the rights and interests of a NATION? destroying all public integrity and patriotism; blasting all faith between man and man; and dooming to endless toil and misery, a poor, because a plundered and misgoverned People!! What is the crime of a pimp and procuress, seducing female virtue to minister to lust, compared with the infamous conduct of those who would seduce the virtue of our citizens, and induce them to sell to a base and plundering faction, that Franchise which they are solemnly bound to use for the best interests of the entire People!

Justice to you, requires that those wretches should be Exposed, and therefore we proceed at once to acquaint you, that a fellow brought from London, wearing Pickwick's spectacles, and carrying a huge Aldermanic cardal, representing himself as the friend, of a friend, of Mr. WOLVERLY ATTWOOD (mark the fellow's cunning and caution) did, yesterday, wait upon Mr. GEORGE BINNS, and make overtures to him, to induce the Chartists to act so as to promote the return of WOLVERLY ATTWOOD.—Mr. Binns, in order to have the fellow's villainous scheme fully developed, and witnessed by others, appointed a second interview with him yesterday afternoon.

This interview took place in the presence of Mr. Williams and several others, who succeeded in drawing him to embody his Proposals in a definite shape; which were, that the sum of ONE HUNDRED & TWENTY-FIVE POUNDS WOULD BE PAID, IF THE CHARTISTS SHOULD ACT AS HE DESIRED.

He was requested to call again at 8 o'clock yesterday evening, and in the meantime arrangements were made for giving the fellow a good tarring and feathering; but, for the sake of the peace of the Town, the latter ceremony was dispensed with. He came at 8 o'clock, when having reiterated his promise, and offering to DEPOSIT THE MONEY, he was then suddenly and terribly convinced of the folly, as well as the iniquity of his conduct. He got such a rebuke as he will not readily forget, and was told to go and tell Mr. Wolverly Attwood, that the Chartists of Sunderland, though poor, were yet honest; while he, though a "highly respectable London Merchant," was yet a most unprincipled scoundrel.

ELECTORS and NON-ELECTORS OF SUNDERLAND:—This statement of facts needs no comment. When such deeds can be practised with impunity under our reformed "Constitution," and the men practising such acts still be recognised as a GENTLEMAN,—the folly of finality and the worth of a gentleman are evident. Let the Franchise be given to all, and its free exercise secured by the BALLOT, & VIRTUE ONLY RECOGNISED AS TRUE NOBILITY—THEN, BUT NOT TILL THEN, WILL ENGLAND BE FREE FROM RESPECTABLE KNAVES—AND ENGLISHMEN BE TRULY HAPPY.

Printed by J. Williams, Bridge Street, Bishopwearmouth.

The Whigs' reply to these speeches came two days later, in a handbill.

### SOURCE 45 'A working man to Mr Attwood'

. . . You pretend to find fault with the new Poor Law; but you did not tell us how to mend it; and I may just tell you, that the less you say about it in Sunderland the better for you and your friends; for I happen to know, that the poor of the parish are much better fed and clothed in the workhouse under the new plan, than they were under the old one.

Mr. Wolverley Attwood, you say you are 'The Poor Man's Friend'. You are Chairman of the 'General Steam Navigation Company.' Your steam-ships have run sailing vessels and sailors all but out of the goods and passenger trades and you are not content with this: you want to increase your gains at the expense of the poor; and the chief reason why you are trying to get into Parliament is to pass a law allowing steam-ships to be navigated without pilots, to save the pilotage; and if you get into Parliament, I have no doubt you and Peel will pass such a law, and immediately throw hundreds of poor pilots out of work into the workhouse.

*A Working Man to Mr Attwood*, 13 September 1841

## Personal attacks

Neither side flinched from making personal attacks on its opponents. The Whigs warned against Tory control of the borough arranged by the retiring MP, Alderman Thompson, in his own interests. The Tories warned against the town falling into the hands of the local Whig families of Grey and Lambton (Handbill 1).

## Canvassing

Both sides canvassed very hard, and it seemed that the result would be close. Attwood therefore decided to try and split Howick's support by encouraging the Chartists to put up their own candidate and by offering £125 towards their expenses. This was done in such a clumsy manner that it was soon made public (Handbill 4 and source 46).

## SOURCE 46 Howick tells in his Journal how the news came to him

Mr Bell brought out with him in the evening Mr Jonassohn a jew & very active politician who came to give me a curious account of an attempt that had been made by a man employed by Attwood to induce the Chartists to put Coll. Thompson in nomination & demand a poll for him, with the view of dividing my supporters. For this purpose the person I have mentioned (his name was Willis & he was the steward of one of Attwood's steamers) offered a certain Mr

# ATTWOOD
### AND
# TORY TREACHERY.

## Independent Men of Sunderland!

You have learned, with indignation and disgust, the details of the detestable plot concocted by the Tories to swamp the Liberal cause,--the CAUSE OF THE PEOPLE--in the Borough of Sunderland, by bringing out a Chartist candidate at the present Election. Happily, most happily, that scheme has been frustrated and admirably exposed, by the talent and stern integrity of Messrs.

### WILLIAMS & BINNS.

Now comes the all-important inquiry, who was the Tory AGENT in this nefarious business, and who was his EMPLOYER?

Wolverly Attwood is the Chairman and Factotum of the "General Steam Navigation Company," one of whose Boats, the "TOURIST," runs between Sunderland and London, under the command of Captain GILBANKS. Before leaving Sunderland last week, Captain Gilbanks announced, that immediately on the vessel's arrival in London, he should return hither to assist in the election of Mr. Wolverly Attwood, his employer. On his way down from town, Captain Gilbanks was seen in company with three other persons at the York Railway Station, where he publicly mentioned the object of their errand, and boasted that though they had no votes, they could *influence* at least THIRTY of the Electors in favour of Mr. Attwood. On Monday, Captain Gilbanks' party made an ostentatious entry into Sunderland in a carriage and four decorated with *red* favours, (Mr. Attwood's London electioneering colours,) one of the *gentlemen*, (a very stout, middle-aged man, in a new olive brown frock coat,) being generally mistaken for Colonel Thompson.

THIS MAN WAS
### *Willis, Steward of Wolverly Attwood's Steamer, "Ocean,"*

And WILLIS, Wolverly Attwood's own Servant, was the AGENT who so basely attempted to buy up the Chartists for his Master!

Who then was Willis's EMPLOYER? The slow-moving finger of Public Scorn points in *one* direction only.

And now, Independent and Honourable MEN of Sunderland, let every one of us ask his Conscience this Question :---
"If I *in any way* support Attwood, am I not accessary to to this horrible villany?"

*Down with Attwood and the TREACHEROUS TORIES!*

Herald Office: R. VINT & CARR, Sunderland.

LEFT: Handbill 5. Attwood and Tory treachery. Attwood was further discredited when news came that one of his employees, Captain Gilbanks, had boasted that he could influence (presumably bribe) 30 voters

Binns the leader of the Sunderland chartists £125 to meet the expenses of going to the poll & obviously also as a bribe, but this offer instead of accepting he rejected with great indignation, having however first by appearing disposed to agree to the proposition made to him got it distinctly made in the presence not only of several of his own friends but of Jonassohn.

Howick, *Journal*

The following day, the Chartist leader George Binns made a public speech exposing what Attwood had tried to do:

### SOURCE 47 Attwood discredited

I have to inform you that at this election, a council of working men—who are consider [ed] incapable of exercising the franchise, have had the manliness and the courage to refuse, with scorn, a bribe for which many of your own electors would have sold their country. (Vociferous cheering.) I will publish to you the history of this transaction. On Monday morning, when we were all expecting the arrival of the Colonel, we observed a carriage and four enter the town at full speed. Every person concluded it was Colonel Thompson. A short time after its arrival, I went down to my shop, and who should I see, but one of these gentlemen who came in the carriage. On ascertaining that my name was Binns, he stated that he wanted to have a little private conversation with me. We went into the parlour. He commenced by telling me that he took a deep interest in this election, and he was very anxious to see Mr. Attwood returned. He wished to know the determination of the Chartists, for he would like to obtain their assistance in returning Mr Attwood. He told me that he had the honour to be acquainted with Mr Job Swain, the Clothier, of Fleet Street, London, and could inform me that he was one of the leading Chartists of London, and exercised a wonderful influence over the Chartists of the metropolis. (Loud laughter.)

He further stated that Job Swain had been the means of inducing the Chartists, almost to a man, to give their support to Mr Attwood. (Renewed laughter.) He stated that he thought we ought to do the same. My reply was this,—'Sir, I have been a long time in the Chartist ranks, I am acquainted with all the Chartist leaders, and I must honestly confess to you that I never heard of this Job Swain before.' (Loud laughter and immense cheering.) I may also tell you that if the Chartists of the South could reconcile the support of Mr Attwood with the great principles we profess, WE COULD NOT; and that we were too far NORTH for that any how.

The next morning, the gentleman called again before breakfast, to know what we were really going to do, and whether Col Thompson was really coming or not, I told him we could not positively tell whether the Colonel would be here or not, 'But, said he, if the Colonel does not come, will you go to the Poll yourself,' 'No, (I replied) to do so would both ruin my business and endanger Colonel Thompson's return at another election,' 'But if a friend of mine in the town,' continued the gentleman, 'was to pay the expenses of the Poll, would you do it THEN?' 'No,' said I, 'it would be wrong of us to receive money from you for such a purpose.' 'When will you know for a certainty whether Col. Thompson will be here,' said he? I replied that we expected a letter that afternoon. He then left me, to call AGAIN. In the mean time I informed the council of what had taken place. I also informed Mr Johnasson. We agreed to meet at my shop, and when the gentleman called at night, I was to introduce them as the Council, and Mr Johnasson as the SECRETARY. We did so, and in the presence of us all, he went over the same ground—and offered to pay us £125 for the purpose stated. This being over, he then was undeceived, he then found out we were too honest to be bought with gold; and he received a severe dressing from Mr Williams, and a severe threat from Mr Johnasson, that if he was not out of the town by 8 o'clock the next morning, his life would be in danger.

Thus ends the affair. (Shouts of 'Down with Attwood and Bribery!') Mr Binns said, 'I will give you his name. It is Mr Willis, Agent of the General Steam Navigation Company, of which Mr Attwood is chairman.' (Loud cheers and laughter.)

Speech by George Binns, 16 September 1841, reported in *The Sunderland & Durham County Herald*

## Polling day and the result

The result was a surprise. Howick describes what happened in his Journal:

### SOURCE 48 Election surprise result

On the Thursday morning I went to Sunderland by eight o'clock just as the poll began. I drove about to try and get some few unpledged voters to vote for me and to visit some of the different polling booths, in every one of which I found things going on better than we could have hoped, by 9 o'clock I had a considerable majority and by ten when I went to breakfast with Hatton Chaytor there was little room for doubt as to the result. My majority went on steadily increasing till the close when the numbers were for me 705 for Attwood 443. I made a short speech announcing this result from the balcony and soon afterwards we went to Ford where there

ABOVE: A recent picture of The Thompson Arms Hotel. Wolverley Attwood made speeches from the balcony of this hotel

was a large party at dinner after which we had again to return to the town for a fancy ball and did not get home and to bed till near one when both Maria and I were dead tired. On Friday the result of the poll was officially declared but I was not allowed to speak by a set of fellows ordered to make a noise; after a great many fruitless attempts to get a hearing I gave it up. Binns was afterwards treated in the same way. Attwood made a speech which was dull and stupid enough but contained not one word of denial of the statement made by Binns though his friends had been boasting that it would be completely disproved, his silence was occasioned by an intimation previously conveyed to him that if he attempted to deny the identity of Willis my friends were ready to prove it. After this the chairing or rather coaching took place for I was paraded all about the town in an open carriage lined with black blue and buff silk and followed by several other carriages. There was an immense display of flags in the procession and a prodigious concourse of people and the whole had passed off as well as possible till just before we got to the place where the procession was to close. A man of the name of Liddle (who keeps a beer shop called the Reform Tavern) with a set of vagabonds who were with him threw some stones and snapped a gun at us. Some of the stones came into the carriage and passed between Featherstonehaugh and myself but without hurting us, they hit however some of the people who followed us and some of those in the carriages behind, particularly Hedworth Williamson who was in Mrs Bell's carriage with her and Ly Howick. The gun also which had been snapped at us was again pointed at them and went off. Luckily it was only loaded with paper and nobody was hurt.

Howick, *Journal*

Of those who supported Howick, 133 had voted for the Tories at the last contested election in 1837, when Alderman Thompson had won. And in 1845, there was a return to the Tories when George Hudson, the 'Railway King' was elected as Tory MP. So how did Howick win in 1841?

Was the election won on the local and national issues? Was Howick the better candidate? Did Attwood lose the election because of his attempts at corruption? Or was there something else?

## Late news

After the election was over, it came out that Howick's supporters had engaged in direct bribery, and particularly 'treating'. Howick was probably ignorant of this. In his Journal he says:

### SOURCE 49 Howick on election conduct

From the beginning I was myself very confident of success, but some of my friends . . . were less so being very much alarmed as to the effect which the . . . expenditure on the other side might produce, there was also a good deal of inclination to follow the example thus set and to spend money in the public houses, but I did all I could to check this and I hope with success.

Howick, *Journal*

In fact Howick's expenditure exceeded £4000 and the national party organiser, Joseph Parkes, had to send his clerk, Hatton, to Sunderland to sort out the debts. Some of these were for 'refreshments' (see the two vouchers on the opposite page)

However, publicans and drinkers were not the only people to benefit from the election; this is made clear in a letter Parkes wrote two years later, to Richard Cobden of the Anti-Corn Law League.

### SOURCE 50 The national party organiser reviews the election

The ribbands, flags, gowns to give away— the Little Drapers' bills—were above £1000. Then the Committee gave away tickets, extensively; though open Treating was not done and few Beer shops regularly opened.

My clerk paid 12 Attorneys an average of £25 each, to settle their claims; and besides

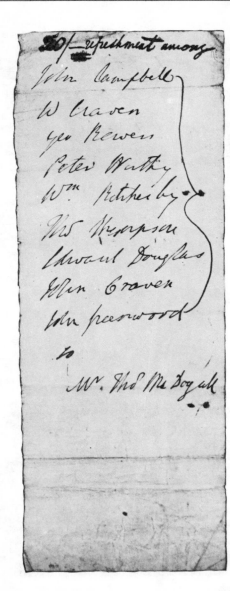

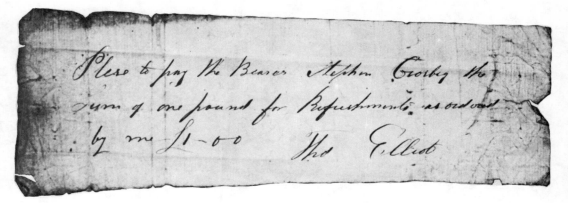

this dozen vermin other 'solicitors' I understand were paid.

In short a more rascally and general illegal and unnecessary expenditure never came before my eyes . . . I don't doubt that this expenditure was an . . . indirect bribery; and that it was resorted to in order to 'influence' the humbler Electorate and the little Shopkeepers; and to counteract a similar practice by the Tories, perhaps exercised to a greater extent . . .

The abuse is an old system in Sunderland. They are old hands and Electioneers, as the Boro' has only been twice uncontested since enfranchised.

Joseph Parkes to Richard Cobden, 12 December 1843, Grey Papers

Population of Great Britain, 1801–1851

| | |
|---|---|
| 1801 | 10 500 000 |
| 1811 | 12 000 000 |
| 1821 | 14 100 000 |
| 1831 | 16 300 000 |
| 1841 | 18 100 000 |
| 1851 | 20 800 000 |

ABOVE AND LEFT: These vouchers show evidence that Howick's supporters had been engaged in corruption. The vouchers entitle the bearer(s) to £1 worth of drinks. It was hoped that gratitude would lead them to vote for Howick

# 2
# The Poor

## Rich and poor

How many really poor people do you know? How do they manage to keep going? If you had lived in the period we are studying, you would have seen much evidence of poverty and even destitution. Life for poor people in, say, the 1830s would have been very different from life for today's poor.

While many of the rich spent their time on leisure activities (sources 51, 52) a large proportion of the population lived in conditions such as those described by the German revolutionary, Friedrich Engels. In his book, *The Condition of the Working Class in England*, he described what he saw in English towns, '. . . a horde of ragged women and children swarm about, as filthy as the swine that thrive upon the garbage heaps and in the puddles . . .

The race that lives in these ruinous cottages behind broken windows or in dark wet cellars in measureless stench and filth . . . must really have reached the lowest stage of humanity!'

The situation was no better—perhaps even worse—in the countryside (source 53). Until the development of government inquiries, many of the middle and upper classes were in fact ignorant of the extent of social problems. Many people, even the poor themselves, accepted poverty as a fact of life and believed that the way out of poverty was through unaided hard work. The only alternatives were to emigrate or to take to crime (sources 54-56).

OPPOSITE: An evening at the opera for the rich
RIGHT: A London slum where the poor crowded together

ABOVE: Emigration from Ireland and
Scotland in particular often involved
the movement of entire communities.
In this contemporary painting, Scottish
emigrants take a last sad look at their
homeland as they set off for Canada
ABOVE RIGHT: A short term solution
for all classes was the
pawnbroker's shop

# Dealing with poverty—the Poor Law system

A system for dealing with poverty, though
inadequate, did exist in the early
nineteenth century. Laws passed in 1597
and 1601 had attempted to deal with the
problem on a local basis. People in any
parish who owned property paid
compulsory rates to unpaid officials known
as the Overseers of the Poor. The
Overseers used the money to look after
the poor who were unable to work—the
aged, sick, young orphans and the
mentally handicapped. Healthy adults,
known as the 'able-bodied poor' were
given relief (money usually) only after
doing some work in the House of

Correction. Some parishes built special
'workhouses' for this purpose. Permission
to look for work in another parish had to
be gained from the Overseers, and if no
work could be found, the pauper was
returned to his or her parish of origin.

In practice this system worked badly.
Overseers were sometimes corrupt,
householders resented paying rates and
many parishes had no workhouse. When
trade was bad and the number of paupers
increased, the Overseers resorted to
schemes which were often well meant but
ineffective and costly. Such schemes did
not encourage people to find work, since
they were destructive to the unemployed
person's will to work (sources 57-59).

## SOURCE 51 Gambling

... To such a height has the spirit of gambling arisen, that at some of the great Tables it is not uncommon to see the stake consist wholly of property in kind. A house of furniture was last week lost to a lady in the neighbourhood of Pall Mall. The successful party had played against it, the stock of a farm in the county of Essex.

*The Times*, 25 September 1797

## SOURCE 52 A dinner for the rich, 1830

**Bill of Fare for eighteen persons**

ABOVE: A middle class family enjoying Christmas dinner

FIRST COURSE:

Puré of Game
Consomée with nouilles
Slices of crimped cod and smelts
Matecore of Carp

*Removes*
Calf's Head
Roast Beef
Turkey with Financier Sauce
Tongue in Chartreuse

*Entrees*
Patty with ragout of Lobster
Partridges with Cabbage, etc.
Fillets of Fowl larded
Turban of Fillets of Rabbit
Cassolettes of Salpeion of Beef Palates
Mutton cutlets
Tendrons of Veal
Lark Patty with Truffles

SECOND COURSE:

Four woodcocks roast
Two Pheasants
Capon garnished with cresses
Partridges roast
Fancy pastry garnished with conserves
Salsify Espagnole sauce
Mushrooms poulette sauce
Punch Jelly
Suedois of Apples
Poached eggs on dressed spinach
Friture of Oysters
Orange Cream

*Removes*
Small camaguins of cheese
Vanilla souflée
Lemon Pudding
Tart of preserved greengages

John Burnett, *Plenty and Want*, Penguin Books, 1968, pp. 84-5

## SOURCE 53 Signs of rural poverty

In the hamlet of Egginston there are twelve tenements belonging to a charity, formed originally out of two barns; these are not always inhabited by paupers of the lowest grade . . . they are generally the resort of persons who are turned out of their houses for non-payment of rents . . . Two only of the tenements have a room upstairs, and all except these two have dirt floors: the other ten tenements consist of one room each. In two or three instances this room is divided by a sort of partition, put up by the inmates. The largest number of persons occupying one of these tenements is eight, viz, a man, his wife and six children, the eldest child aged sixteen, the youngest an infant.

There is no bed in the house, the whole family sleeping on two heaps of straw confined in two corners of the room by stakes driven into the ground; none of the tenements are ceiled; there are no back doors, nor windows for ventilation; the filth is thrown out into the stagnant pools in front of the tenement; the stench is at all times great . . . with the exception of one, the rest of the tenements are occupied by families with children of all ages. The number of persons in the whole is 55.

C. E. Tonna, *The Perils of the Nation*, 1844, pp. 158-9

ABOVE: In Ireland, evicted families lived in roadside hovels such as this
LEFT: A row of colliers' cottages in Northumberland. These houses had two floors, but many agricultural workers' cottages had no upstairs accommodation

## SOURCE 54 How to succeed

Energy enables a man to force his way through irksome drudgery . . . it is not . . . talent that is required to ensure success in any pursuit, so much as purpose—not merely the power to achieve, but the will to labour . . . perseveringly. Even if a man fails in his efforts, it will be a great satisfaction to him to enjoy the consciousness of having done his best. In humble life nothing can be more cheering and beautiful than to see a man combatting suffering by patience . . .

Samuel Smiles, *Self-Help*, London, 1859, p. 42

## SOURCE 55 The Sheepstealer

I am a brisk lad and my fortune is bad,
Oh, and I am most wonderful poor;
Now indeed I intend my fortune to mend
And to build a house down on the moor, My brave boys,
And to build a house down on the moor.

In my meadow I'll keep fat oxen and sheep
And a neat little nag on the downs;
In the middle of the night when the moon do shine bright,
There's a number of work to be done.

I'll ride all around in another man's ground
And I'll take a fat sheep for my own;
Oh, I'll end of his life by the aid of my knife
And then I will carry him home.

My children shall pull the skin from the ewe
And I'll be in a place where there's none;
When the constable do come, I'll stand with my gun
And swear all I have is my own.

R. Palmer (ed), *The Painful Plough*, Cambridge University Press, 1973, p. 36

ABOVE: An army of street sellers made a bare living by selling anything from dog collars to nutmeg graters. In difficult times they would have to appeal for poor relief

ABOVE: A refuge for the destitute. The male ward in a shelter

### SOURCE 56 Poverty and crime

In the House of Correction, at Brixton, more than one half of the number of prisoners were lately found to be under twenty-one. The causes of the evil may be briefly told. Nothing tends more powerfully than pauperism to weaken the natural affections and destroy the sense of parental obligation . . . Of the crowds of boys who inhabit our prisons and infest our streets the depravity of an immense proportion may be traced to the neglect and criminality of their natural protectors.

*Quarterly Review*, Vol. XXXVII, p. 492

### SOURCE 57 Labour rate and roundsman system

In some parishes the distance between setting the poor to work on parish works and setting them to work in private industry was bridged by the Labour Rate and the Roundsman systems. In the first, the ratepayer agreed to employ and pay wages to a number of labourers, the number being assessed according to his rental, or real property. In the Roundsman system the parish paid the employers to employ paupers at rates fixed by the Parish as appropriate to the pauper's needs.

S. E. Finer, *The Life and Times of Sir Edwin Chadwick*, Methuen, 1952, p. 40

### SOURCE 58 Thomas Gilbert's Act, 1782

XXXII. And be it further enacted, that where there shall be . . . any poor person or persons who shall be able and willing to work, but who cannot get employment, it shall and may be lawful for the guardian of the poor of such parish . . . to agree for the labour of such person or persons . . . and to maintaining or cause such person or persons to be properly maintained, lodged and provided for, until such employment shall be procured, and during the time of such work, and to receive the money to be earned by such work or labour, and apply it on such maintenance, as far as the same will go, and make up the deficiency if any.

W. C. Glen, *The Statutes in Force Relating to the Poor*, London, 1857, pp. 117-8

## SOURCE 59 The Speenhamland solution

A meeting of the magistrates for the county [Berkshire] was held about Easter 1795, when the following plans were submitted to their consideration: 1st, that the magistrates should fix the lowest price to be given for labour, as they were empowered to do . . .; and secondly, that they should act with uniformity, in the relief of the impotent and infirm poor, by a Table of universal practice . . . The first plan was rejected . . . but the second was adopted, and the Table [below] was published as the rule for the information of magistrates and overseers.

| Income should be | for a Man | For a Single Woman | For a Man and his Wife | With One Child | With Two Children |
|---|---|---|---|---|---|
| When the gallon loaf is 1s 0d | 3s 0d | 2s 0d | 4s 6d | 6s 0d | 7s 6d |
| When the gallon loaf is 1s 1d | 3s 3d | 2s 1d | 4s 10d | 6s 5d | 8s 0d |
| When the gallon loaf is 1s 2d | 3s 6d | 2s 2d | 5s 2d | 6s 10d | 8s 6d |
| When the gallon loaf is 1s 3d | 3s 9d | 2s 3d | 5s 6d | 7s 3d | 9s 0d |
| When the gallon loaf is 1s 4d | 4s 0d | 2s 4d | 5s 10d | 7s 8d | 9s 6d |
| When the gallon loaf is 1s 5d | 4s 0d | 2s 5d | 5s 11d | 7s 10d | 9s 9d |
| When the gallon loaf is 1s 6d | 4s 3d | 2s 6d | 6s 3d | 8s 3d | 10s 3d |
| When the gallon loaf is 1s 7d | 4s 3d | 2s 7d | 6s 4d | 8s 5d | 10s 6d |
| When the gallon loaf is 1s 8d | 4s 6d | 2s 8d | 6s 8d | 8s 10d | 11s 0d |
| When the gallon loaf is 1s 9d | 4s 6d | 2s 9d | 6s 9d | 9s 0d | 11s 3d |
| When the gallon loaf is 1s 10d | 4s 9d | 2s 10d | 7s 1d | 9s 5d | 11s 9d |

*Loaf weighing 8 lb 11 oz*

F. M. Eden, *The State of the Poor*, London, 1797, Vol. I, p. 576

This shows us one part of what should be the Weekly Income of the Industrious Poor, as settled by the Magistrates for the county of Berkshire, at a meeting held at Speenhamland, 6 May, 1795.

BELOW: Agricultural workers saw threshing machines as a particular threat. Hand threshing with a flail was usually winter work, when other work was scarce

ABOVE: Robert Owen who emphasised the values of the cooperative ideal and planned economy

RIGHT: A contemporary cartoon looks into the future and comments on the possible results of the population growth of the period

## After the wars with France

Conditions were especially difficult during the wars with France of 1793-1815. There were bad harvests and it was difficult to import corn, and so there was a steep price rise in the labourers' staple food, bread. Even though there was plenty of work and wages were rising fast, prices of all commodities were rising even faster, and this meant that the buying power of wages was in fact falling. This brought extra pressure on the Poor Law system; even people in employment often failed to make ends meet (sources 60, 61).

At the end of the war, things became worse. There was a slump in industry and in agriculture, and with an ever-growing number of people wanting work, employers could offer low wages. For its part the Government, representing the interests of the landowners, may have made the situation worse. They refused to allow the import of cheap corn from the Continent until the price of British wheat was as high as famine level prices (sources 62, 63).

As economic distress grew, so did social discontent. There were outbreaks of rioting in East Anglia in 1816, and this clear danger signal prompted some people to see poverty and its relief in a new light. How could things be improved?

Many unemployed workers saw the introduction of machinery as the cause

of poverty. Machines seemed to take work away from people, and so it was felt that getting rid of them would mean plenty of manual work, and therefore put an end to poverty. Others believed that the problem of poverty would be solved when political reform had been achieved. People like Robert Owen believed that poverty would be beaten only when society itself was organised differently (sources 64-66). His book, *A New View of Society*, describes the changes he made at New Lanark in Scotland. No children under nine were employed, and the workers were decently housed. Streets were cleaned, and shops sold goods at reasonable prices. And to the surprise of other employers, Owen made a profit out of this venture.

But the man whose ideas carried most weight at this time was the Reverend Thomas Malthus. His *Essay on Population* (1798) warned of the dangers of population growth overtaking the means of subsistence. He also commented on the poor law system, claiming that it did little to help people in the long term sense. It was his belief that if people received too much outdoor relief too easily, they would be careless of the future and would burden the nation through early marriages which produced yet more paupers. Malthus was prepared to see the abolition of compulsory poor relief.

It was these ideas and the ideas of men like Malthus which were particularly attractive to householders who seemed to pay more each year in poor rates. However, what was to be done? Discussion brought no action (sources 67, 68).

**SOURCE 60 Annual average gazette price of British wheat per quarter 1801-51**

| | s | d | | s | d | | s | d | | s | d | | s | d | | s | d |
|---|---|---|---|---|---|---|---|---|---|---|---|---|---|---|---|---|---|
| 1801 | 119 | 6 | 1810 | 106 | 5 | 1819 | 74 | 6 | 1828 | 60 | 5 | 1837 | 55 | 10 | 1846 | 54 | 8 |
| 1802 | 69 | 10 | 1811 | 95 | 3 | 1820 | 67 | 10 | 1829 | 66 | 3 | 1838 | 64 | 7 | 1847 | 69 | 9 |
| 1803 | 58 | 10 | 1812 | 126 | 6 | 1821 | 56 | 1 | 1830 | 64 | 3 | 1839 | 70 | 8 | 1848 | 50 | 6 |
| 1804 | 62 | 3 | 1813 | 109 | 9 | 1822 | 44 | 7 | 1831 | 66 | 4 | 1840 | 66 | 4 | 1849 | 44 | 3 |
| 1805 | 89 | 9 | 1814 | 74 | 4 | 1823 | 53 | 4 | 1832 | 58 | 8 | 1841 | 64 | 4 | 1850 | 40 | 3 |
| 1806 | 79 | 1 | 1815 | 65 | 7 | 1824 | 63 | 11 | 1833 | 52 | 11 | 1842 | 57 | 3 | 1851 | 38 | 6 |
| 1807 | 75 | 4 | 1816 | 78 | 6 | 1825 | 68 | 6 | 1834 | 46 | 1 | 1843 | 50 | 1 | | | |
| 1808 | 81 | 4 | 1817 | 96 | 11 | 1826 | 58 | 8 | 1835 | 39 | 4 | 1844 | 51 | 3 | | | |
| 1809 | 97 | 4 | 1818 | 86 | 3 | 1827 | 58 | 6 | 1836 | 48 | 6 | 1845 | 50 | 10 | | | |

D. Layton & S. Crowther, *The Study of Prices*, Macmillan, 1935, p. 234

## SOURCE 61 Two family budgets in 1794

### A Banbury labourer

The family consists of a widower between 50 and 60 with two daughters aged 21 and 13 and a son, 7 years old. The elder daughter was sick and looked after the house. The younger daughter went to school and the boy earned nothing.

|                                        | £   | s  | d |                   |
|----------------------------------------|-----|----|---|-------------------|
| Earnings (weekly)                      |     | 8  | 0 | for 48 weeks      |
|                                        |     | 9  | 0 | for 4 weeks       |
| Weekly Parish allowance for children   |     | 2  | 0 |                   |
| Expenses (yearly)                      |     |    |   |                   |
|     Bread          | 13  | 13 | 0 |                   |
|     Tea and sugar  | 2   | 10 | 0 |                   |
|     Butter and lard| 1   | 10 | 0 |                   |
|     Beer and milk  | 1   | 0  | 0 |                   |
|     Bacon and other meat | 1 | 10 | 0 |               |
|     Soap, candles etc. |   | 15 | 0 |                 |
|     House rent     | 3   | 0  | 0 |                   |
|     Coal           | 2   | 10 | 0 |                   |
|     Shoes and shirts | 3 | 0  | 0 |                   |
|     Other clothes  | 2   | 10 | 0 |                   |

### A Wolverhampton spectacle frame maker

The family consists of a man (40 years old) his wife and four children; viz. boys of ten and seven, girls of two and six months.

|                                        | £   | s  | d |
|----------------------------------------|-----|----|---|
| Earnings (yearly)                      | 49  | 9  | 4 |
| Expenses (yearly)                      |     |    |   |
|     84 stones of flour | 10 | 4 | 9 |
|     12 lbs meat per week | 10 | 8 | 0 |
|     butter, cheese | 4   | 11 | 0 |
|     milk           | 1   | 6  | 6 |
|     small beer     | 1   | 6  | 6 |

| | | | |
|---|---|---|---|
| strong beer | 2 | 13 | 0 |
| vegetables | 4 | 0 | 0 |
| tea, sugar, soap, candles | 5 | 0 | 0 |
| rent | 6 | 0 | 0 |
| taxes | | 10 | 0 |
| shoes and clothing | 4 | 10 | 0 |

Adapted from Eden, *State of the Poor*, Vol. II, pp. 585, 661

## SOURCE 62 Depression and surplus labour

These Manchester yeomen and magistrates . . . have always treated the working people in a most abominable manner. I know one of these fellows who swears, 'Damn his eyes, 7/- a week is plenty for them', that when he goes round to see how much work his weavers have in their looms, he takes a well-fed dog with him . . . for the purpose of insulting them by the contrast. He said some time ago that 'The sons of bitches had eaten up all the stinging nettles for 10 miles round Manchester, and now they had no greens to their broth.' Upon my expressing indignation, he said 'Damn their eyes, what need you care about them? How could I sell you goods so cheap if I cared anything about them?'

Francis Place to J. C. Hobhouse, 20 August 1819

## SOURCE 63 An argument against cheap corn

Let us imagine that the opening of our ports to the foreign grower might end in bringing into this country a permanent annual supply of 10 000 000 of quarters of corn; this would . . . bring about an increase in our manufacturing population to the amount, we will say, of 3 000 000 workmen employed in fabricating commodities to be exported in exchange for this corn. We should thus have, within the limits of the country, 3 000 000 manufacturers entirely dependent upon foreign countries for employment and subsidence.

*Quarterly Review*, Vol. XXXVII, p. 426

ABOVE: Bread riots in London, 1815, protesting against the Corn Laws which kept the price of corn, and therefore bread, high

ABOVE: An exhibition of steam engines. Most could be adapted to drive machinery

BELOW: Robert Owen's New Lanark Mills in Scotland. Here Owen put into effect his ideas on the way society should be organised

## SOURCE 64 A view of machinery and poverty

The extent to which the employment of machinery has been pushed as a substitute for human labour has, at length, brought on a new crisis . . . our manufacturers . . . overflow with workmen, for whose industry there is no profitable demand. The employment of machinery not only stops the gap through which the surplus of our agricultural population has been used to make its way into manufactures, but it has likewise thrown out of employment a considerable proportion of hands which had been previously occupied in the fabrication of wrought commodities . . .

*Quarterly Review*, Vol. XXXVIII, p. 428

## SOURCE 65 Political reform and the relief of poverty

14th. That the passing of corn laws in opposition to the express will of the people—the combination act, in order to prevent work people from unitedly attempting to raise their wages in proportion to the advancement of provisions—and the imposing a duty on foreign wools, at a time when the woollen manufacture, and those employed therein, are in the most deplorable condition—appear to this meeting, proof positive, that until the Members of the Commons House are really appointed by the people at large, little improvement is to be expected in the circumstances of the people, or diminution of their distress.

Resolution passed at the Meeting held on Hunslet Moor, 19 July 1819

## SOURCE 66 A cure for poverty

Under this view of the subject, any plan for the amelioration of the poor should combine means to prevent their children from acquiring bad habits, and to give them good ones—to provide useful training and instruction for them—to provide proper labour for the adults—to direct their labour and expenditure so as to produce the greatest benefit to themselves and to society; and to place them under such circumstances as shall remove them from unnecessary temptations, and closely unite their interest and duty.

These advantages cannot be given either to individuals or to families separately, or to large congregated numbers.

They can be effectually introduced into practice only under arrangements that would unite in one establishment a population of from 500 to 1500 persons, averaging about 1000 . . .

Robert Owen, 'Report to the Committee of the Association for the Relief of the Manufacturing Poor', March 1817

ABOVE: A contemporary view of what Owen's ideas would mean if carried out

## SOURCE 67 A hard line attitude

The labouring poor . . . seem always to live from hand to mouth. Their present wants employ their whole attention, and they seldom think of the future . . . All that is beyond their present necessities goes, generally speaking, to the ale-house. The poor-laws of England may therefore be said to diminish both the power and the will to save among the common people, and thus to weaken one of the strongest incentives to sobriety (soberness) and industry, and consequently, to happiness . . .

   The evil is perhaps gone too far to be remedied, but I feel little doubt in my own mind that if the poor-laws had never existed, though there might have been a few more instances of very severe distress, yet that the aggregate mass of happiness among the common people would have been much greater than it is at present.

Rev. T. R. Malthus, *Essay on Population*, 1798, pp. 86–7, 91–4

## SOURCE 68 The cost of looking after the poor

| Years | Total sum levied | Sums expended for the Relief of the Poor |
| --- | --- | --- |
| Average of 1748-49-50 | £730 135 | £689 971 |
| 1776 | £1 720 316 | £1 521 732 |
| Average of 1783-4-5 | £2 167 748 | £1 912 241 |
| 1803 | £5 348 204 | £4 077 891 |
| 1812-13 | £8 640 842 | £6 656 105 |
| 1817-18 | £9 320 440 | £7 890 148 |
| 1820-21 | £8 411 893 | £6 958 445 |

Select Committee on Poor Rate Returns, *Report V* Appendix A, 1828

# The Government acts

People like Malthus believed that governments had no business meddling in such matters as the relief of poverty (source 69). Indeed, in Scotland for example, help for the poor was largely in the hands of the State Church, and there was no obligation for parishes to collect poor rates unless the church felt it necessary. Even the reforming Act of 1845 avoided making poor rate assessment compulsory, and poorhouses existed only where it was believed they would be useful. However, in England and Wales, where paying poor rates was compulsory, the increasing cost of relief led to Government investigations in 1817 and again in 1824. No conclusions were reached and nothing was done. Abuses in the system remained, and costs continued to rise.

Then in 1830 serious riots broke out in the agricultural districts of the south. The continuing grinding poverty of rural workers and the unwillingness of anyone in authority to tackle problems of high prices, erratic employment and low wages led these men to use violent protest in an attempt to obtain some remedy (sources 70-72).

Public alarm at the riots forced the government to attempt some final solution to the poor law problem.

ABOVE: A contemporary cartoon comments on the Swing Riots, as the rural disturbances of 1830 came to be known. A man said to be called Captain Swing was supposed to be behind all the unrest and destruction

ABOVE: Edwin Chadwick. Tall, strong and with great powers of endurance, He worked a twelve hour day for 20 years. Chadwick trained as a lawyer, but became disillusioned with the law when he had to defend a bigamist he knew to be guilty. He subsequently worked as a journalist and then became involved in social reform. His main motivation was efficiency and hatred of waste

## The Royal Commission on the Poor Laws

The Whig Government was unable to take immediate action because it was so involved with the struggle over the First Reform Bill, and so in 1832 it set up a Royal Commission to look into the operation of the Poor Law System. Questionnaires were sent out and replies were received from about 10 per cent of the English and Welsh parishes.

The Report which came out in 1834 was largely the work of Nassau Senior, an Oxford professor, and Edwin Chadwick, a Manchester-born lawyer. Chadwick in particular became identified with the law that was passed as a result of the Commission's Report. This was because it was largely his ideas which dictated the Report's recommendations.

Once published, the Report became popular reading. The evidence it contained supported what some people knew and many people suspected. It showed how the cost of providing poor relief had been rocketing; it demonstrated the inefficiency of paying allowances through schemes like the Speenhamland and Roundsmen systems; and it pointed to the inefficiency and corruption of local systems of administration (sources 73-75).

Chadwick was most appalled by the waste which resulted from this system, especially the way the subsidised poor competed with independent workers on the labour market. It was his hope that whatever laws resulted from the

Commission's enquiry would have the effect of forcing paupers back onto the labour market where they would have to survive by their own efforts (source 76).

The way to do this, he recommended, was to abolish relief for all able-bodied people not living in workhouses. And so that people did not flock to the workhouses, these places should be made as unpleasant as possible, so that the inmates would be kept in conditions 'less eligible' (more miserable) than the poorest independent worker (sources 77, 78).

To implement this scheme, the Report suggested a central Board which would regulate the system and attempt to enforce some kind of national uniformity.

No consideration was given in the Report to the *causes* of poverty.

## The Poor Law Amendment Act

This Act, the result of the Commission's Report, became law in August 1834. Its main concern was to set up a central body in London to administer the relief of poverty on a national basis. Three paid Government Commissioners and a paid Secretary were appointed. These four men formed the Central Poor Law Department, and its job was to guide the local Poor Law officers in their duties.

Chadwick, who became the Department's first Secretary, had hoped that the Commissioners would have greater powers, but Parliament was cautious. In the localities the unpaid Overseers were to be replaced by Boards of Guardians, elected by the ratepayers of parishes that were grouped together into Poor Law Unions.

As far as dealing with poverty was concerned, the Act was rather vague. Outdoor relief was not abolished, as the Report had suggested, but beyond this it was assumed that the Commissioners would work along the lines of the Report (source 79).

This they did. And at the core of the Report had been the workhouse and the principle of 'less eligibility'.

### SOURCE 69 Government interference

And one of the principle objections to [the poor laws] is that for this assistance which some of the poor receive, in itself almost a doubtful blessing, the common people of England is subjected to a set of grating, inconvenient and tyrannical laws, totally inconsistent with the genuine spirit of the constitution.
*Annual Register*, 1830, pp. 199-200

### SOURCE 70 Riots in the south, 1830

From the latter end of October, the southern counties were kept in a state of great alarm. Stacks and farm buildings were set on fire during the night, and these atrocities extended into Cambridgeshire and the eastern district of the island.

The peasantry, too, in many places, particularly in Hampshire, Wiltshire, Kent and Berkshire, assembled in tumultuous crowds, in order to obtain an increase of wages; destroyed mills and other machinery; and proceeded to other acts of outrageous violence.
*Annual Register*

### SOURCE 71 The Duke of Wellington goes hunting

I induced the magistrates to put themselves on horseback, each at the head of his own servants and retainers, grooms, huntsmen, gamekeepers, armed with horsewhips, pistols, fowling pieces and what they could get, and to attack in concert, if necessary, or singly, these mobs, disperse them, and take and put in confinement those who could not escape. This was done in a spirited manner, in many instances, and it is astonishing how soon the country was tranquillised, and that in the best way, by the activity and spirit of the gentlemen.
In E. J. Hobsbawm & G. Rudé, *Captain Swing*, Lawrence and Wishart, 1970, p. 255

*Now you little rascal, I'll give you your choice either to stop by your handy work and be roasted, or come with me and be hanged a little bit.*

THE SWING CATCHER GENERAL AT HIS AVOCATION

ABOVE: The Swing catcher

## SOURCE 72 Aftermath of the 1830 riots

In all, 1976 prisoners were tried by 90 courts sitting in 34 counties. We may briefly tabulate the sum total of their sentences as follows:

| | |
|---|---|
| Sentenced to death: | 19 |
| Transported | 505 (of these only 481 sailed) |
| Prison | 644 |
| Fined | 7 |
| Whipped | 1 |
| Acquitted or bound over | 800 |

Hobsbawm & Rudé, *Captain Swing*, p. 262

## SOURCE 73 Poor Law costs

It is true . . . that for the year ending the 25th March 1832, the total amount of the money expended for the relief of the poor [is] higher than for any year since the year 1820 . . .

*Report . . . into the Administration and Practical operation of the Poor Laws*, 1834, p. 54

## SOURCE 74 The wastefulness of the roundsman system

In many parishes, especially in Oxfordshire, I have seen the Roundsman and Ticket system adopted, as the best means of conveying to the pauper that amount of income which the parish has determined to be his due . . . This scheme recommends itself peculiarly to the selfishness and shortsighted jealousy of the farmers; amongst whom every man's eye is on his neighbour, lest by any means his portion of the . . . burden should have been unduly lightened; many a farmer has dismissed labourers from profitable employment, in order, as he imagined, to make others assist in maintaining them.

*First Annual Report of the Poor Law Commissioners*, 1835, p. 211

## SOURCE 75 How the Overseers operated

As a body, I found annual overseers wholly incompetent to discharge the duties of their office, either from the interference of private occupations, or from a want of experience and skill; but most frequently from both these courses. Their object is to get through the year with as little unpopularity and trouble as possible, their successors therefore, have frequently to complain of demands left unsettled, and rates uncollected, either from carelessness or a desire to gain the trifling popularity of having called for fewer assessments than usual. In rural districts the overseers are farmers; in towns generally shopkeepers; and in villages usually one of each of those classes.

Asst Commissioner S. Walcott, North Wales, *Royal Commission on the Poor Laws, Report Appendix A, Part 2*, 1834

## SOURCE 76 A modern historian's view of Chadwick

Unlike a Shaftesbury or a Howard, his . . . devotion was not to this poor woman or that unhappy child, but to the public at large. His characteristic emotion was not pity or love, but indignation and anger. His motive was neither religious nor benevolent—it was horror of waste.

Finer, *The Life and Times of Sir Edwin Chadwick*, p. 3

## SOURCE 77 Abolishing outdoor relief

Throughout the evidence it is shown, that in proportion as the condition of any pauper class is elevated above the condition of independent labourers, the condition of independent class is depressed . . . such persons, therefore, are under the strongest inducements to quit the less eligible class of labourers and enter the more eligible class of paupers . . .

We therefore submit . . .

FIRST, THAT EXCEPT AS TO MEDICAL ATTENDANCE . . . ALL RELIEF WHATEVER TO ABLE BODIED PERSONS OR TO THEIR FAMILIES, OTHERWISE THAN IN WELL-REGULATED WORKHOUSES . . . SHALL BE DECLARED UNLAWFUL, AND SHALL CEASE.

*Report of the Royal Commission into the Poor Laws*, 1834 (1905 edition), p. 228

ABOVE: Mob burning a farm in Kent

E

ABOVE The women's yard in a workhouse. The 1834 Report hoped there would be separate facilities for the sick, the aged, mentally ill, and children. In fact the only division was between the sexes

## SOURCE 78 The workhouse system

By the workhouse system is meant having all relief through the workhouse, making this workhouse an uninviting place of wholesome restraint, preventing any of its inmates from going out or receiving visitors, without a written order to that effect from one of the overseers, disallowing beer and tobacco, and finding them work according to their ability; thus making the parish fund the last resource of the pauper, and rendering the person who administers the relief the hardest taskmaster and the worst paymaster that the idle and the dissolute can apply to.

*Report of the Royal Commission into the Poor Laws, 1834, p. 29*

## SOURCE 79 What the Act said about relief for the able-bodied

And whereas difficulty may arise in case any immediate and universal remedy is attempted to be applied in the matters aforesaid (outdoor relief for the able-bodied); be it further enacted, from that and after the passing of this Act, it shall be lawful for the said commissioners . . . to declare to what extent and for what period the relief to be given to able-bodied persons or to their families . . . may be administered out of the workhouse.

*Glen, The Statutes in Force Relating to the Poor, p. 399*

LEFT: This is a diet from a workhouse which was operating before 1834. Compare it with the following diet suggested in the Poor Law Commission's Second Annual Report (1836):

Breakfasts—6 oz bread and 1½ oz cheese

Dinners—Sundays 5 oz meat and ½ lb potatoes
Tuesdays and Thursdays ditto
Other days 1½ pints soup

Supper—days on which there was meat for dinner, 6 oz bread and 1½ pints broth; other days, 6 oz bread and 2 oz cheese

The diet of the paupers in the house shall, for the present, be as follows:

| DAY OF WEEK. | BREAKFAST. | DINNER. | SUPPER. |
|---|---|---|---|
| MONDAY, | Milk and Oatmeal, with six oz of Bread. | Peas Porridge, with four ounces of Bread. | Milk and Oatmeal, with four ounces of Bread. |
| TUESDAY, | Ditto, | Rice Frumenty, with four ounces of Bread. | Ditto. |
| WEDNESDAY, | Ditto, | Ox Head Stew, with four ounces of Bread. | Ditto. |
| THURSDAY, | Ditto, | Six ounce of boiled Beef Potatoes, and four oz. of Bread. | Beef Broth, with four oz. Bread. |
| FRIDAY, | Ditto, | Eight ounces hot Rolls, with Treacle. | Milk and Oatmeal, with four ounces of Bread. |
| SATURDAY, | Ditto, | Rice Frumenty, with four ounces of Bread. | Ditto. |
| SUNDAY, | Ditto, | Six ounces of boiled Beef, Potatoes, and four oz. of Bread. | Beef Broth, with four oz. Bread. |

# The Poor Law in operation

## Workhouses

Some unions of parishes had to build new workhouses like the one shown on this page. Others continued to use buildings which had been built in the eighteenth century or earlier.

Inside, the workhouses were uninviting places. This fitted in with the Commissioners' ideas about making life more miserable for paupers than for the poorest independent labourer. Accommodation was basic, and so was food. Inmates were carefully watched and there were strictly enforced rules. Misdeeds were punished. And so that paupers would not breed more paupers, there was complete segregation of the sexes. This meant that while they were in a workhouse, families were broken up (sources 80-83).

In spite of this grim picture of workhouse life, people who were completely destitute were given shelter and food, there was some care of the sick, and some attempt to educate adults so that they could support themselves. While criticising the unsuitability of pauper schools, the educationist Sir James Kay-Shuttleworth provides evidence that some pauper children might have benefited from the basic education provided in a workhouse (source 84).

## The success of the system

People who were not paupers thought the new system was very successful. In

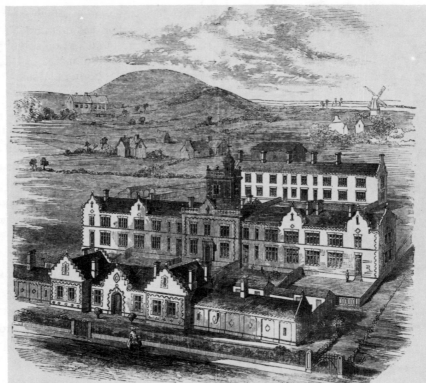

### SCARBOROUGH NEW WORKHOUSE.

AMONG the improvements lately carried out in Scarborough is workhouse, which has recently been erected, situated in Dean-street, leading to the Cemetery. The group of buildings will accommodate from two hundred to three hundred inmates. The front range is for boardroom, offices, &c.; the entrance gateway forming a pleasing feature, being composed of moulded white bricks with a bold keystone over, which is a large shield with the Scarborough arms carved in high relief. The governor's apartments occupy a central position, and are so arranged that he possesses the fullest command of, and is in the closest approximation with, every ward of the establishment. These apartments are also crowned by a tower which furnishes a very efficient system of ventilation. The infirmary at the back is appropriately on the highest part of the ground (being nearly twenty feet higher than the front), and is thoroughly well lighted and ventilated; and, although the building, as a whole, is free from the expensive ornamental decoration that too often characterises similar establishments, it possesses, from the artistic mixture of brickwork, a most attractive and substantial appearance. The whole of the buildings are well supplied with water and lighted with gas; and these advantages, coupled with a capital system of drainage, make the sanitary regulations all that could be desired. The works have been erected from designs furnished by Messrs. George and Henry Styan, architects, York, under whose direction they have been successfully carried out.

ABOVE: The new Scarborough workhouse—grand enough to appear in the *Illustrated London News*

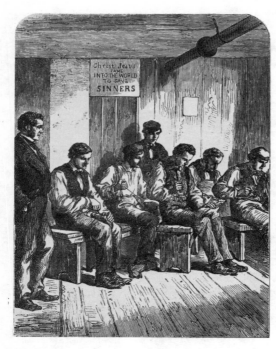

ABOVE: Some workhouses took seriously the opportunity to re-educate paupers to a trade

RIGHT: An artist's impression of a workhouse dinner

particular, they liked the way in which the cost of running poor relief was met and controlled. In addition, it was felt by some that the new poor law system had a beneficial effect on the labouring classes. It improved their morals and made them better workers (sources 85-88).

However, these views were not shared by everyone.

## SOURCE 80 'Less eligibility'

Although we have . . . endeavoured to give the inmates of workhouses an adequate supply of nutritious food, we have not been insensible to the danger which would result from the impression that they were better off, as respects food, than the independent poor; and we have endeavoured to prevent this impression, by excluding from the dietary anything in the nature of luxuries.

*Report of the Further Amendment of the Poor Law*, 1839, p. 50

## SOURCE 81 Food arrangements

So they established the rule, that all poor should have the alternative (for they would compel nobody, not they) of being starved by a gradual process in the house, or by a quick one out of it. With this view, they contracted with the waterworks to lay on an unlimited supply of water; and with a cornfactor to supply periodically small quantities of oatmeal; and issued three meals of thin gruel a day, with an onion twice a week, and half a roll on Sundays.

Charles Dickens, *Oliver Twist*, London, 1838, p. 24

## SOURCE 82  Workhouse punishments

| Name | Offence | Date of Offence | Punishment inflicted by Master or other officer |
|---|---|---|---|
| Twenty-nine women at the mill | Neglecting and refusing to work | 24th July 1851 | Dinner and supper milk stopped |
| Owen Trainor | Stealing onions | 1st September 1851 | Flogged |
| James Acheson | Going to town without permission | 14th February 1852 | Six hours in lock-up |
| James Close | Refractory conduct | 14th February 1852 | Six hours in lock-up |
| Francis Campbell John Burns | Absconding with Union clothes | 1st December 1853 | Flogged |
| Mary Carroll | Refusing to work and damaging her clothes | 8th November 1854 | 9 hours in lock-up |
| Mary Carroll | Persisting in refusing to work | 9th November 1854 | 7 hours in lock-up |

Offences and Punishment Book of Newry Workhouse, Northern Ireland Record Office

ABOVE: Another view of women's quarters in a workhouse

## SOURCE 83  An official statement

As regards the separation of families . . . it is obviously impossible to provide for the cohabitation of married couples in a public establishment, with any regard to decency, without giving a separate apartment to each couple—an arrangement, the expense of which would preclude its adoption; and which would create other . . . difficulties as to order, discipline, and cleanliness in the workhouse.

*Report on the Further Amendment of the Poor Law*, 1839, p. 51

ABOVE: Dr Guthrie, educationalist, minister and philanthropist, teaching his 'ragged school'

### SOURCE 84 Pauper schools

The great object to be kept in view in regulating any school for the instruction of the children of the labouring class is the rearing of hardy and intelligent men . . .

An orphan or deserted child, educated from infancy to the age of 12 or 14 in a workhouse, if taught reading, writing or arithmetic only, is generally unfitted for earning his livelihood by labour.

Poor Law Commission, *Report on the Training of Pauper Children*, 1841, pp. 33-4

### SOURCE 85 The cost of poverty, 1837

A table showing the amount of Money expended for the Relief and Maintenance of the Poor, during the Years ended Easter, 1803, and 25th March, 1818 and 1837; specifying the Amount, Rate per cent, and Rate per head, of Decrease in 1837, as compared with the Years 1803 and 1818 respectively—the former being the Year in which the smallest, and the latter of the Year in which the largest, sum of Money was expended for the Relief of the Poor for which the authentic Parliamentary Returns have been received.

Population in 1801   8 872 980
Expended for Relief, &c.   £4 077 891
of the Poor during the
Year ended Easter 1803

Population in 1821   11 978 875
Expended for Relief, &c.   £7 870 801
of the Poor during the
Year ended 25th March, 1818

Population in 1831   13 897 187
Expended for Relief, &c.   £4 044 741
of the Poor during the
Year ended 25th March, 1837

| | |
|---|---|
| Decrease in 1837, compared with 1803 | 1% |
| Decrease in 1837, compared with 1818 | 49% |
| Expenditure in 1803, with reference to Population 1801 | 9s 2d per head |
| Expenditure in 1818, with reference to Population 1821 | 13s 2d per head |
| Expenditure in 1837, with reference to Population 1831 | 5s 10d per head |
| Decrease in 1837, compared with 1803 | 3s 4d per head |
| Decrease in 1837, compared with 1818 | 7s 4d per head |

*Third Annual Report of the Poor Law Commissioners*, p. 311

### SOURCE 86 The moral effect of the new system

The positive good which has been wrought by the new Poor Law is, in the first place, that the public houses and beer-shops are, without question, much less attended than before: that drunkenness is decidedly less frequently seen, and I think practised; and that, as I do not believe any increase has taken place in the number of robberies committed in this part of the country, to supply the lacking means to the worse part of our pauper population they are driven to be more moral and more domestic characters than before.

Evidence of the Rev. Dr Wrench, Minister of Salehurst, in *Second Annual Report of the Poor Law Commissioners*, 1836, p. 227

## SOURCE 87 Support for the new Poor Law

### Highworth and Swindon Union

At a meeting of the Board of Guardians held at Highworth, on Wednesday the 11th of January, 1837, the following Resolutions were moved, seconded, and carried unanimously:

That the Board regard with peculiar satisfaction the working of the Poor Law Amendment Act, during the twelve months it has been in operation in this Union of sixteen parishes, and 12 611 population.

That the pecuniary savings of the ratepayers, since the formation of the Union, as compared with the average expenditure of the three preceding years, is upwards of 54 per cent per annum.

That this large reduction has not been accomplished by causing privation to the aged or infirm, or the really necessitous and deserving poor, but by economy in the general management, and by the removal of those opportunities for imposition which existed under the old law; and this pecuniary saving is also attended with decided symptoms of returning industry among the labouring poor, and it is evident that the new law is working a great moral improvement in the habits of this class of people.

Signed by order of the Board,

A. S. Crowdy, Clerk of the Union

*Third Annual Report of The Poor Law Commissioners*, pp. 182-3

## SOURCE 88 The success of the system

Persons who never could be made to work before have become good labourers, and do not express any dissatisfaction with the measure. In most parishes the moral character of the poor is improving; there is a disposition to be more orderly and well-behaved. So far as I can judge, from the inquiries I have made from time to time, and from conversations with respectable farmers and others, who hold no offices, I may venture to say that the measure is working very satisfactorily; that the great body of the labouring poor throughout the Union have become reconciled to it; that the workhouse is held in great dread; that there is a greater disposition to seek for employment, and but very few complaints of misbehaviour; and that cases of bastardy are on the decline.

Evidence of Langham Rokesby Esq., Chairman of the Market Harborough Union; in the *Second Annual Report of the Poor Law Commissioners*, p. 31

## How the Poor Law was received

The Poor Law Commission started work in the south of England, where the main problem was long-term rural poverty. Unions were formed from groups of 15-20 parishes, and since this was a period of fine summers, good harvests and plenty of work, the new system was accepted by the labouring population. Where there was opposition, it was often worked up by 'parties who benefited by former abuses!' (source 89).

However, when at the end of 1836 the Commissioners decided to introduce the system into the north of England, a surprise awaited them.

### Opposition in the north

In the industrial north, employment varied according to fluctuations in trade. This often meant that huge numbers of workers might be out of work, but for a relatively short time. For these people, the old system of a short period on dole money seemed better than having to go into a workhouse. On the other hand, if there was a long trade depression the numbers involved would choke the workhouses (source 90).

Opposition to the new poor law system was speedily organised. The existing movement for factory reform provided leadership in men like Richard Oastler from Huddersfield, John Fielden the Todmorden cotton manufacturer, and Joseph Rayner Stephens a non-conformist preacher. Local Anti-Poor Law committees were formed and emotional meetings and publications whipped up a

RIGHT: Richard Oastler, the social reformer

frenzy of hatred for the new workhouses—the Bastilles as they became known (sources 91-93).

The fact that local magistrates and newly-appointed poor law guardians supported the opposition forced the Commissioners to proceed carefully. Although much of the Anti-Poor Law support put its energy into Chartism, the relief of poverty remained a very sensitive issue in the north. Sporadic riots continued into the 1840s, and local boards continued to provide outdoor relief for the able-bodied (source 94).

**The end of the Commission**
Opposition in the north made things difficult for the Commission. In addition the national press, and especially *The Times*, campaigned against the growing power of the three Commissioners. Inside the Commission there were personality clashes and Chadwick, its energetic Secretary, began to get more involved in the public health question.

In 1842 Parliament granted the Commission a further five-year term, but in reducing the number of Assistant Commissioners from twelve to nine it caused an overloading of work which affected morale. When the Andover Union scandal broke in 1845, the Poor Law Commission was in no condition to defend itself (source 95).

The Parliamentary Select Committee which investigated the Andover case was strongly critical of the Poor Law Commission. In 1847 the Home Secretary announced it would not continue. In its place a Poor Law Board was created, with a President who was to be a Member of Parliament with a place in the Government.

This meant that the relief of poverty entered the sphere of party politics. However, attitudes to poverty did not change and ideas about dealing with it still rested on the 1834 Report. Government continued to assume throughout the nineteenth century that poverty was the result of laziness and bad habits: self-help was still the key to improvement. The causes of poverty remained a mystery.

LEFT: Joseph Rayner Stephens, minister and political agitator

ABOVE: A mother and child outside a factory

### SOURCE 89 Opposition in Devon

Your orders . . . have here, as elsewhere, excited opposition amongst those parties who benefited by former abuses. The leaders of the opposition are to be found amongst the constant overseers (gentlemen accustomed to accept the office for £15 a year, and quit it with a well-furnished purse); the little shop keeper, at whose house the poor were paid, and who received the amount of old debts and encouraged new, from which the pauper never got free; the beer-shop keeper, at whose house great part of the relief was expended; and the little farmer or the lime-kiln owner, whose influence at the vestry enabled him to pay one half his labour from the parish funds, under the name of relief in aid of wages.

Evidence of W. J. Gilbert, in the *Second Annual Report of the Poor Law Commission*

### SOURCE 90 Erratic employment

It is well known that the cotton manufacture of this kingdom has been long and greatly depressed, and that numbers of persons engaged in it have been thrown out of employment, and great distress occasioned in the various towns and districts of which it is the staple manufacture.

The borough of Stockport, . . . has suffered, in common with other towns, from its general and long-continued depression.

. . . Several thousand persons have been thrown out of employment, who still remain without any prospect of being able to return to it.

Of the established at work, a great part are so only partially; and the working of short time (that is, of four days per week) has been continued since May last.

W. Cooke Taylor, *Notes of a Tour of the Manufacturing Districts of Lancashire*, 1842

### SOURCE 91 Huddersfield Anti-Poor Law Committee address

Fellow Rate Payers,

The time has come for you to give a practical demonstration of your hatred to the new Starvation Law.

Recollect! that the 25th March is the day which is set apart for the election of new Guardians for the ensuing year; therefore it will depend upon your exertions, whether you will allow men to be elected as Guardians, who are the mere tools of the three Commissioners in carrying out their diabolical schemes for starving the poor, reducing the labourers' wages and robbing you the rate-payers of that salutary control you have hitherto exercised over your money and your township's affairs; or will you elect men of character and of humanity, whose high and independent spirit will scorn to submit to the three headed monster of Somerset House, and will prefer death itself, rather than sacrifice the rights of their neighbours and constituents at the bidding of three pensioned lawyers, residing in London, and living in princely splendour out of your hard-earned money . . .

Therefore for the guidance of your conduct, we beg to suggest to you the following considerations:

First—We recommend the formation of local committees in every township, village, and hamlet, where committees have not been formed.

Ratepayers, do your duty and select none who are in the remotest degree favourable to the hellish Act. Remember that the law is cruel, illegal, and unconstitutional—one of degradation and absolute starvation for the poor. That the real object of it is to lower wages and punish poverty as a crime. Remember also that children and parents are dying frequently in the same Bastile, without seeing one another, or knowing of one another's fate.

*Northern Star*, 10 March 1838

## SOURCE 92  The cruelty of the new Poor Law

Remember, always that liberty—freedom from confinement as well as food and clothing—is the birthright of every Englishman, however poor. What, Sir, is the principle of the New Poor Law? The condition imposed upon Englishmen by that accursed law is, that man shall give up his liberty to save his life! That, before he shall eat a piece of bread, he shall go into prison, under circumstances which I shall speak of hereafter, in prison he shall enjoy his right to live, but it shall be at the expense of that liberty, without which life itself becomes a burden and a curse . . .

Thank God the law of the land does not yet say—though the Commissioners of the New Poor Law have dared to say—that poverty is a crime, by which an Englishman may be deprived of the blessings of liberty.

R. Oastler, *The Rights of the Poor to Liberty and Life*, Liverpool, 1838, pp. 5-6

### SOURCE 93 What to do in Newcastle

The people were not going to stand this, and he would say, that sooner than wife and husband, and father and son, should be sundered and dungeoned, and fed on 'skillee',—sooner than wife or daughter should wear the prison dress—sooner than that—Newcastle ought to be, and should be—one blaze of fire, with only one way to put it out, and that with the blood of all who supported this abominable measure . . .

Report of a speech by the Rev. J. R. Stephens, in Gammage, *History of the Chartist Movement*, p. 64

### SOURCE 94 Riots in the north

All the manufacturing districts have been up in arms; at Preston the insurgents were fired upon and some of them wounded mortally. At Stockport where there are upwards of 20 000 persons out of employment who have no resources but those of plunder and beggary, a large body of rioters broke open and pillaged the workhouses of food and clothing, and mobs robbed the provision shops.

*Illustrated London News*, August 1842

RIGHT: The Stockport riots, 1842

**SOURCE 95 The Andover workhouse scandal:**
**the evidence of Charles Lewis, labourer**

*What work were you employed about when you were in the workhouse?*
I was employed breaking bones.
*Were other men engaged in the same work?*
Yes . . .
*During the time you were so employed, did you ever see any men gnaw anything or eat anything*
*from these bones?*
I have seen them eat marrow out of these bones . . .
*Have you often seen them eat the marrow?*
I have.
*Did they state why they did it?*
I really believe they were hungry.
*Did you yourself feel extremely hungry at this time?*
I did, but my stomach would not take it.
*You could not swallow the marrow?*
No.
*Did you see any of the men gnaw the meat from the bones?*
Yes.
*Did they use to steal the bones and hide them away?*
Yes.

Report of the Select Committee on the Andover Union, 1846, p. 104

# Emigration after 1815

## Introduction

The statistics on this page show that a steady flow of emigrants left Britain in the first half of the nineteenth century. As we shall see, the decision to try and start life again in another country was not an easy one to make, and the difficulties and dangers of a voyage to Canada or New Zealand were not to be taken lightly. So there had to be a good reason for wanting to emigrate.

If you were able to ask emigrants of 1820 why they decided to leave Britain, they would probably have mentioned some of the following reasons:

The population was growing fast, so in many places there were shortages of food, houses and jobs.
Sometimes bad harvests made food scarce, and terrible hardship resulted. Unemployment became serious after the French Wars (1793-1815). Soldiers and sailors came home looking for jobs at a time when agriculture and industry had entered a depression. In some rural areas work was even harder to find, especially during the winter, as farmers introduced labour-saving threshing machines.
Some people were looking for an escape—from the law, their work, the climate, their families or the political system.

But there had always been some people looking for an escape; bad harvests had not been infrequent, and after previous

| Total emigration from Great Britain, 1815–1854 | |
|---|---|
| 1815–1819 | 97 799 |
| 1820–1824 | 95 030 |
| 1825–1829 | 121 084 |
| 1830–1834 | 381 956 |
| 1835–1839 | 287 358 |
| 1840–1844 | 465 577 |
| 1845–1849 | 1 029 209 |
| 1850–1854 | 1 638 945 |

Destination of Emigrants from U.K.

| | Canada | USA | Australia/ New Zealand | South Africa | Elsewhere |
|---|---|---|---|---|---|
| 1821 | 12 995 | 4 958 | 320 | No | 384 |
| 1831 | 58 067 | 23 418 | 1 561 | Figures | 114 |
| 1841 | 38 164 | 45 017 | 32 625 | Available | 2 786 |
| 1851 | 42 605 | 267 357 | 21 532 | | 4 472 |

FAR LEFT: Irish peasants search for potatoes during the potato famine. Thousands were to die through hunger and disease

LEFT: Paupers at work at stone-breaking in a workhouse

wars there had been unemployment and hard times. So why did many more people than ever before choose to emigrate in the years following the Napoleonic wars? One thing that was new was the rate at which the population was increasing, but that would not have mattered if the amount of food and the number of jobs had kept pace with the population growth.

In the past when people had been threatened by starvation and unemployment they had not emigrated, or at least not in large numbers. The fact was that in the nineteenth century life in another land was seen as an alternative to death at home. Not only had colonies been established already, so that something was known about what was involved in going to live overseas, but there were regular shipping lines, at least across the Atlantic. At the same time transport at home was improving and with better roads it was possible for people living inland to get to the ports.

We should not assume that all those who emigrated were down-and-outs, those for whom life at home had nothing to offer. Some of those who went in search of a new life overseas were already quite well off. Others had been earning enough to save up the money for the passage and to see them through their early weeks in a new land. Another thing we must not assume is that, because of the improvements already mentioned, it would have been easy to emigrate. For most people it was not. To move anywhere new is to take risks; many of you will know that from your own experience of moving from one area of this country to another. You can't be certain before you go that you will like the new place better than the old, that you will find new friends to make up for leaving the old ones behind. Imagine the emigrants of the early nineteenth century feeling the kind of apprehension any of us might feel, but also not being certain whether they would be able to find a home and job, or whether they would survive the journey.

There were certainly attractions about going to a new country; for the unemployed the prospect of work, for those who wanted to be their own masters the opportunity to buy a plot of land and farm independently, and for all the prospect of a new start and the excitement of the unknown. But it was not an easy decision to take and we must try to imagine why, for more and more people, the attractions proved stronger than the fears and reported horrors of the journey across the Atlantic or, even worse, all the way to Australia or New Zealand.

# Attitudes and opinions

### Government opinion
There was official support for the poor to emigrate, both in England and abroad. In 1826 a Select Committee on Emigration from the United Kingdom published its first report. It pointed out:

### SOURCE 96 The Government encourages emigration

That there are extensive districts in Ireland, and districts in England and Scotland, where the population is at the present moment redundant; in other words, where there exists a very considerable number of able-bodied and active labourers, beyond that number to which any existing demand for labour can afford employment.

That the effect of this redundancy is ... to deteriorate the general conditions of the labouring classes ...

BELOW: A cartoonist's view of what would happen if emigration continued unchecked

That in England, this redundant population has been in part supported by a parochial rate ...

That in the British Colonies in North America ... at the Cape of Good Hope, and in New South Wales, and Van Diemen's Land, there are tracts of unappropriated land of the most fertile quality, capable of receiving and subsisting any proportion of the redundant population of this country, for whose conveyance thither, means could be found at any time, present or future.

From the *First Report of Select Committee on Emigration from the United Kingdom*, 1826

### Attitudes amongst ratepayers
Many property owners were also keen that the poor should emigrate. If you look again at Source 68 in the section 'The Poor' you will see how the cost of looking after the poor had rocketed. And, of course, the money was collected from local rate payers. Getting rid of some of the poor to Canada or Australia—or anywhere— would mean that property owners would not have to pay so much in poor rates.

# Help for emigrants
However strong the reasons for emigration were in theory, an unemployed man who was already having difficulty in keeping himself and his family was in no position to find the money to get to the port, pay for his passage and then for his keep for some weeks before he found a new job. Often the people who would most benefit from emigrating were those who could least afford to do so. As the government was in favour of emigration it was decided that finance should be given in certain cases to help groups of people who wished to leave the country. Similarly, some landlords offered money to labourers on their lands to help pay the cost of the passage to a colony abroad. In other areas, Emigration Committees were established to help groups of would-be emigrants in a particular parish.

Sometimes particular types of people were helped. From 1835 a free bounty of £20 was given to young married mechanics and agricultural labourers who wished to emigrate to Australia. By the 1830s single women were very much in demand and special incentives were offered to them:

## SOURCE 97 Young women wanted

### NOTICE TO YOUNG WOMEN
Desirous of bettering their conditions by an emigration to New South Wales

In New South Wales and Van Diemen's Land there are very few women compared with the whole number of people, so that it is impossible to get women enough as Female Servants or for other Female Employments. The consequences is, that desirable situations, with good wages, are easily obtained by Females in those countries; but the passage is so long that few can pay the expence of it without help. There is now, however, the following favourable opportunity of going to New South Wales.

The Committee has been formed in London for the purpose of facilitating emigration, which intends to send out a ship in the course of the Spring, expressly for the conveyance of Female Emigrants, under an experienced and respectable Man and his Wife, who have been engaged as Super-intendents. The parties who go in that vessel must be Unmarried Women or Widows; must be between the ages of 18 and 30; and must be of good health and character. They must also be able to pay £6 towards the expense of their passage. The remainder of the expense will be paid by the Society. Every arrangement will be made for the comfort of the Emigrants during the voyage; ... they will also be taken care of on their first landing in the Colonies; and they will find there, ready for them, a list of the different situations to be obtained.
*Incentive for Female Migrants,* 1833.

In many cases, however, the money given by Committees, landlords or the State was not sufficient to cover all the emigrant's expenses. Usually it barely covered the cost of the journey. Once in a new country some emigrants were completely abandoned without a penny and the poor of one country became the poor of another.

## Where should they go?

Once the idea of emigration became a possibility in people's minds, they had to face the question of where to go. This was a very different business from looking at glossy holiday brochures and deciding on the most attractive place they could afford, as we do now. In only one respect it was similar: any advertisements were published by people trying to sell and persuade, so it was unlikely that snags or difficulties would be mentioned. For many people there was in practice little choice of destination; they simply went where the local Committee arranged for them to go, or else they went to join friends or relatives. To some extent of course their decision depended on their motives for emigrating at all. If they were going in search of work then they must go to an area where people with their skills were needed: it would be no good a miner going to a place where only agricultural labourers could find employment.

In the first part of the century the vast majority of British emigrants went to Canada. What made them decide to go there?

## SOURCE 98 A contemporary observer on the kind of people who should be drawn to North America

As to the classes to which British America offers inducements to emigrate, much will depend upon individual character . . . The settlers who thrive soonest are men of steady habits, accustomed to labour.

Practical farmers possessing from £200 to £600 may purchase in any of the Colonies farms with from twenty to thirty acres cleared, which may be cultivated agreeably to the system of husbandry practised in the United Kingdom . . .

Joiners, stonemasons, saddlers, shoemakers, tailors, blacksmiths, cart, mill and wheel-wrights, and (in the seaports), coopers may always find employment. Brewers may succeed, but in a few years there will be more encouragement for them. Butchers generally do well. For spinners, weavers, or those engaged in manufactures, there is not the smallest encouragement.

Young men of education, clerks in mercantile houses, or shopmen, need not expect the least encouragement, unless previously engaged by the merchants or shopkeepers in America. Many young men, however, by persevering minds, and industrious habits, have baffled every obstacle, and finally succeeded in establishing themselves in trade. Many of the richest merchants in the Colonies were of this description . . .

H. A. Innis & A. R. Lower (ed), *Select Documents in Canadian Economic History 1783–1855*, Toronto, 1933, p. 42

## Making decisions

Making a decision to emigrate was difficult in itself. But it was also necessary to think about where to go, whether the journey could be afforded, and if not, whether local help might be expected. Friends and family would be left behind, the journey might end in disaster, and having arrived at their destination wretched living conditions and unemployment might be waiting for them. And yet, on the other hand they might find success and happiness

For some, the decision to emigrate was considered carefully ; for others it was taken in sheer desperation. Many were taken in by the misleading advertisements which appeared in contemporary newspapers ; they had no way of knowing whether the advertising was reliable or not. Inevitably, there were men ready to take advantage of their ignorance.

### SOURCE 99 Villains abroad

Men of broken fortunes, or unprincipled adventurers, were generally the persons who have been engaged in the traffic long known as the 'white slave trade' of transporting Emigrants to America. They travelled over the country among the labouring classes, allured them by flattering, and commonly false, accounts of the New World, to decide on emigrating, and to pay half of the passage-money in advance. A ship of the worst class, ill-found with materials, and most uncomfortably accommodated, was chartered to a certain port, where the passengers embarked; crowded closely in the hold, the provisions and water indifferent and often unwholesome and scanty; inhaling the foul air generated by filth and dirt—typhus fever was almost inevitably produced, and as is too well known many of the passengers usually became its victims.

Innis & Lower (ed) *Select Documents in Canadian Economic History 1783–1885*, p. 192

In deciding to emigrate many people were ignorant of the consequences of their choice. They did not always realise that the cost of the passage itself was often only a fraction of the total cost. There was a small network of people waiting to take money from the unsuspecting emigrant. Brokers, usually working for shipping companies, made money according to the number of passages they sold. In many towns they had agents who advertised cheap passages, but when the intending emigrants arrived at the ports they often found they had to wait several days for the ship to sail (waiting so that as many passengers as possible could be crammed on board). Runners (agents' men) would 'persuade' the waiting emigrants to stay in particular boarding houses and buy food from certain shops.

It is hard to imagine that if people had been aware beforehand of the horrors that awaited them at the ports (at Liverpool in particular), or the miseries and hazards of the voyage, that they would ever have taken the decision to go.

# Emigration from Sussex

We have seen already that people had different motives for emigrating. However, by examining a particular part of the country, it will be possible to look in detail at an interesting example of a community deciding to emigrate.

## Social unrest and emigration

Sussex is a mainly rural county, and so the agricultural depression which followed the French wars had serious effects in that area. The situation failed to improve in the 1820s, and by the end of the decade social unrest boiled over into rioting amongst agricultural workers. Farm labourers demonstrated against low wages and the fact that new techniques like mechanised threshing were taking away their jobs. In the south east, rioting began in Kent and spread from there to West Sussex. In November 1830 there was a disturbance at the workhouse in the village of Petworth and two days later, fires broke out at villages nearby.

Farm labourers wanted relief from tithes, lower rents and higher wages. In many cases farmers gave in to their demands, but they too were in financial difficulties. They were forced to pay high taxes and rates and until they had some relief from these it would always be difficult to pay higher wages.

In these circumstances, emigration seemed to offer a way out. It was

ABOVE: Emigrants huddle on the quayside with their belongings, waiting for a ship

believed that if some labourers and paupers could be persuaded to leave the country, work would be more freely available, and there would be fewer paupers in the workhouse to be kept at the rate-payers' expense.

In 1832 the principal land owner at Petworth, Lord Egremont, decided to take action.

## From Petworth to Upper Canada

Lord Egremont lived in Petworth House and owned much of the surrounding land including a proportion of the village. In 1832, in order to help relieve the hardship of the agricultural labourers in the area, he set up the Petworth Emigration Committee. The Committee chairman was the local vicar, the Rev. Thomas Sockett. With the money that Lord Egremont had

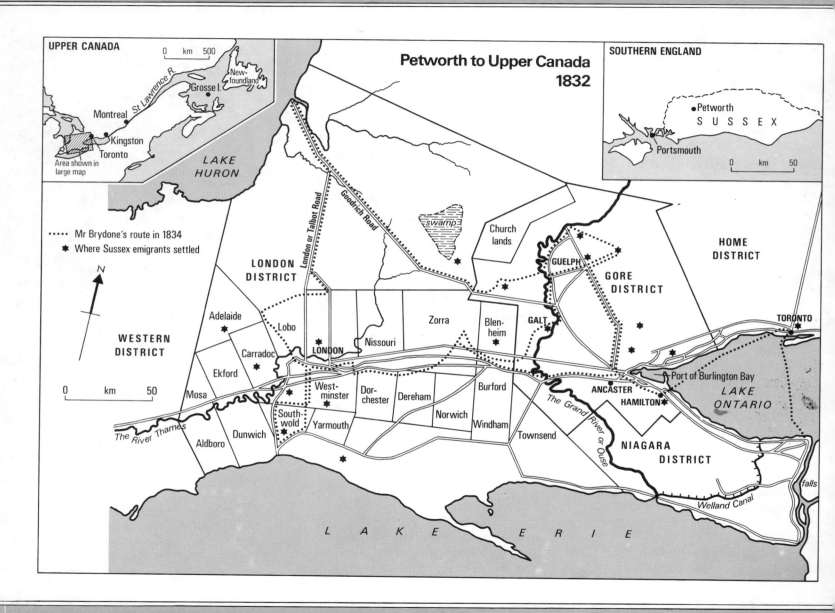

**Petworth to Upper Canada 1832**

UPPER CANADA

0   km   500

Newfoundland

St Lawrence R.

Grosse I.

Montreal

Kingston

Toronto

Area shown in large map

LAKE HURON

SOUTHERN ENGLAND

Petworth

SUSSEX

Portsmouth

0   km   50

······ Mr Brydone's route in 1834

✷ Where Sussex emigrants settled

N

WESTERN DISTRICT

LONDON DISTRICT

London or Talbot Road

Goodrich Road

swamp

Church lands

GUELPH

GORE DISTRICT

HOME DISTRICT

Adelaide

Lobo

Zorra

Blenheim

GALT

TORONTO

Carradoc

LONDON

Nissouri

Ekford

Westminster

Dorchester

Dereham

Burford

ANCASTER

Port of Burlington Bay

LAKE ONTARIO

Mosa

Southwold

Yarmouth

Norwich

Windham

HAMILTON

The Grand River or Ouse

0   km   50

The River Thames

Aldboro

Dunwich

Townsend

NIAGARA DISTRICT

Welland Canal

falls

L A K E   E R I E

donated for the Committee's use, Sockett organised a scheme for assisting individuals who wished to emigrate to Canada from Petworth and the surrounding villages. The scheme turned out to be very successful and an example to other landowners. However, we should remember that the Petworth scheme was an exception rather than the rule, since few emigrants in other parts of the country received the sort of help given to the Petworth emigrants.

---

### List of Necessaries for Emigrants to UPPER CANADA.

| Families should take their | Single Men must have |
|---|---|
| Bedding. | A Bed or Mattress. |
| Blankets. | Metal Plate or wooden Trencher. |
| Sheets, &c. | Some kind of Metal Cup or Mug. |
| Pewter Plates or wooden Trenchers. | Knife, Fork and Spoon. |
| Knives and Forks and Spoons. | |
| Metal Cups and Mugs. | *All, or any of which, may be procured at* |
| Tea Kettles and Saucepans. | *Portsmouth, if the Parties arrive there* |
| Working Tools of all descriptions. | *unprovided.* |
| (A large tin Can or watering pot would be useful) | |

Besides various other portable Articles in domestic use (especially of metal) according as Families may be provided. A Cask, not exceeding the size of a Hogshead or 60 Gallons, affords an excellent and dry case, for packing such Articles as are not likely to be wanted 'till the end of the voyage. All packages should be marked with the Owner's name, in large Letters. *One* hundred weight of Luggage is allowed to be taken by each Individual above 14 years of age.

*The following is the lowest outfit recommended to Parishes for their Laborers.*

| | |
|---|---|
| A Fur Cap. | Two Jersey Frocks. |
| A warm great Coat. | Four Shirts. |
| A Flushing Jacket and Trowsers. | Four pairs Stockings. |
| A Duck Frock and Trowsers. | Three pairs Shoes. |
| A canvas Frock & two pairs of Trowsers. | A Bible and Prayer Book. |

Women in the same proportion, especially a *warm Cloak.*

*All the above may be purchased at Petworth.*

It is also a matter of great importance, that Emigrants should take with them a good Character, (if they should have the happiness to possess one,) fairly written and well attested, also Copies of Marriage or Baptismal Registers, or any other Certificates or Papers likely to be useful; the whole to be inclosed in a small Tin Case.

J. Phillips, Printer, Petworth.

---

## The Emigration Committee in action

In March 1832, the Committee issued a pamphlet called 'Information To Persons Desirous Of Emigrating From This Neighbourhood To Upper Canada'. This told hopeful emigrants about the assistance offered by Lord Egremont and the Committee, what life in Canada would be like, and it also told them how much money each family would have to raise for the journey. As the list of interested people grew, handbills began to appear throughout the area giving details of sailing dates and telling emigrants what they should take with them.

Conditions in Sussex made the decision to emigrate a fairly easy one to make. It was aided by the knowledge that the Emigration Committee would give support and that Thomas Sockett had made arrangements with the Canada Land Company that land should be available for sale when they arrived. Emigrants could also see how leaving the country would help those who stayed behind, for in the short term local trade had already increased. Sockett had given redundant shoemakers the job of making shoes for the emigrants, and local traders benefited from all the other needs of the emigrants.

During 1832 and 1833 four ships left Portsmouth carrying emigrants from Petworth and surrounding villages. In these two years 970 people left the area. The majority were agricultural labourers, but there were also included: 1 artist, 2 blacksmiths, 13 bricklayers, 2 brickmakers, 2 butchers, 7 carpenters, 2 farmers, 6 gardeners, 1 landscape painter, 1 miller, 1 house painter, 3 army pensioners, 1 printer, 9 sawyers, 2 schoolmasters, 8 shoemakers, 1 tailor, 2 turners, 1 weaver, 1 woolstapler, 2 wheelwrights, 1 widow and 14 single women.

## Mr Brydone and the *British Tar*

In 1834 the Committee sent out another party of emigrants. Each previous ship had been equipped with a doctor and a superintendent whose job it was to supervise the party and escort them to their destinations. In 1834 the superintendent chosen by Thomas Sockett and the Committee was James Marr Brydone. Mr Brydone was a naval doctor who had once farmed in Scotland and had travelled to Australia. Sockett writes in the Minute Book of the Committee that he felt they were 'very fortunate' to have engaged such a competent and experienced man.

Mr Brydone was to convey the party of emigrants from Petworth to York (now called Toronto), Upper Canada. Sockett's instructions were very clear:

OPPOSITE: Emigration from Sussex to Upper Canada in the 1830s

LEFT: List of necessities for emigrants to Upper Canada. (One of the handbills circulated in the area by Petworth Emigration Committee)

## SOURCE 100 Mr Brydone receives instructions

On arriving at York, U.C., Mr Brydone will first communicate with A. B. Hawke, Esq, the government agent for emigrants in that city, who will probably attend him to wait on the Governor. From Mr Hawke, Mr Brydone will receive the best information and such assistance as may be necessary, towards forwarding the emigrants to the different places, to which they may wish (having friends already settled there) to proceed, or which may be recommended to them by the Government, as likely to afford advantageous locations, or profitable employment.

The Committee wish to recommend to Mr Brydone's peculiar care, on their arrival at York, U.C., any boys, or lads, who may be placed under his charge, and who do not belong to any families going out, and to use every effort in his power, towards placing them with masters of good character, and, where practicable, getting them apprenticed. Mr Brydone is requested to keep a particular account of the destination of the different families, and individuals, and to communicate the same to the Committee.

Emigration Committee Year Book, 1834

Mr Brydone kept a careful account of the entire journey for the Petworth Committee. All the following extracts are taken from his account. He begins with a detailed description of the ship, which may help us to imagine what the voyage must have been like:

## SOURCE 101 Mr Brydone's own account of the voyage

*The British Tar*, A.I., 383 Tons, commanded by Captain Robert Crawford, had been taken up by the Committee, for the conveyance of emigrants to Montreal, and had been fitted up, in a substantial manner, with a double row of berths, six feet square, the whole length of the vessel from the partition, or bulkhead of the Captain's cabin, to that which bounded the space for the seamen.

A partition was built across the ship, before the main hatchway, and another the main mast, by which, the portion appropriated to the emigrants, was divided into three parts, each having its own separate access, namely by the fore, main and aft hatchways.

The division forward was appropriated to the boys above fourteen years of age and single men: the other two to the families: the partition between which, was so constructed as to give a separate water closet to each of three divisions, thereby avoiding the risk, and inconvenience, especially to females and children, or others in delicate health, attendant on going on deck in bad weather, and at the same time securing perfect cleanliness and comfort.

By this arrangement, either of these divisions could if required have been readily appropriated as intermediate berths to persons rather above the common class, or, in the event of sickness during the voyage, become a place of complete separation.

No berths were placed across any of the partitions. The whole centre of the ship was left free, except a small store-room, for the convenience of issuing the provisions.

BELOW: This ship was called the *Bourneuf* and took passengers to Australia. Like the *British Tar* it was well planned, but it often carried too many people. On one voyage, 83 people died from disease

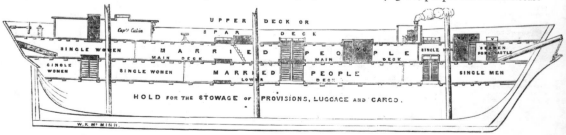

It at once struck me, that these arrangements were excellent, and such as ought to be adopted on board every ship carrying emigrants.

James Marr Brydone, *Narrative of a Voyage . . . to Toronto . . .*, 1834

There were various rules and regulations intended to keep the ship clean and safe and a rota of jobs was drawn up for the men on board. The men responsible for

seeing that the ship was clean were also to prevent smoking between decks, swearing or improper conduct of any sort'.

Food was carefully rationed—but adequate, as you can see from the 'Scale of Victualling' shown on this page.

At the end of the voyage, Mr Brydone commented:

The provisions were remarkably good; all continued to the last, in an excellent state of preservation.

Many of the families admitted that the daily allowance was more than sufficient, all the people spoke of their superior quality, and several of the young men expressed a wish that the voyage might last for six months.

Brydone, *Narrative*

Mr Brydone's account of the first ten days at sea gives a good idea of life on board:

**Sunday, April 20th**—Read prayers, and the sermon which had been addressed to the Emigrants, on board the Lord Melville and Eveline, in 1832, by the Rev T. Sockett, Rector of Petworth.

The same wind with which we sailed from Portsmouth, continued until the 26th April, by which time, we had reached the long. of 36,47 having run nearly half our distance. At noon the sun obscure: calm, foggy weather, with constant rain and heavy seas.

The ship rolling much, the coppers were upset before dinner, without other injury than that of dirtying the beef, and frightening John Barton, the cook, whose post was immediately filled by Job Hodge. In the evening, the wind sprung up from the N.W. and increased to a strong gale in the night.

**Sunday, April 27th**—At 4 a.m. wind N. moderate breeze, and clear weather. Read prayers. Lat. 46.3; long. 37.8.

The morning of the 28th April brought us an increase to our party, Mrs Ditton having been safely put to bed of a girl.

The lead pipe from the water closets was choked up through carelessness; the carpenter, in endeavouring to clear it of a large bone, injured the pipe so much, as to render its removal necessary, and reported that he could not repair it. In this dilemma two young men (Kemps) voluntarily brought their knowledge and labour to our aid, and repaired it in a substantial manner. The lead which had been used was much too thin; and I mention the circumstances by way of precaution, on any future occasion, as there is

scarcely a greater privation on board of an Emigrant ship, than the loss of this kind of accommodation.

**April 29th**—A violent gale, the wind blowing very hard from the West, from the attention however, of Captain Crawford to the ship, and still more from the qualities of the ship herself, we rode safely, and triumphantly, through the storm; and the people suffered but little comparative inconvenience. From this period, the winds continued alternately adverse and favourable.

Finding that all the people, more especially those affected by sea sickness, were suffering much from thirst and cold during this tempestuous weather; and that the latter was increasing as we approached Newfoundland, and knowing, from experience, that the water on board of a ship, is at no time a very palatable beverage, I procured some peas from Captain Crawford, and caused to be made for every person a pint of excellent soup, which was so generally liked, that I was induced to continue it, every Tuesday and Saturday, until we reached the river St. Lawrence.

Brydone, *Narrative*

In the next fortnight the christening of the Dittons' baby, the sight of icebergs and of other ships seem to have been the only notable events. Then, on 14 May, 'at 3 p.m. discovered the high ground of Newfoundland. The people were rejoiced at the sight of land, but nothing flattered by its snow covered mountains'

The only illnesses any of the emigrants suffered from during the voyage were seasickness and measles (there were twelve cases—none of them serious). It was not surprising that Mr Brydone was annoyed that the ship should have been held up by quarantine regulations at Grosse Isle. He found it impossible to 'describe how sorry I was to see a cleanly and healthy people mixed, as they were, in the dirt and filth of thousands.' He was even more upset that they were instructed to throw all the straw from the beds overboard, when they still had ten days' travelling to Toronto ahead of them. And in addition to the inconvenience the delay (lasting nine days) cost £60.15s.0d.

From Montreal a new boat took the party to Kingston, and from there they travelled to Toronto by steam boat. Mr Brydone was evidently pleased with their progress in the later stages of the journey:

**June 13th,** at 8 a.m. arrived at Kingston, six miles from Kingston Mills; having, notwithstanding the accidental delays, arising from various causes; and in no slight degree, from the impediments, presented by stumps and floating trees, which I trust will not long be suffered to remain, accomplished the passage from Montreal to Kingston in seven days.

All the people arrived there in perfect health, for altho' from the dismal stories spread abroad of the extreme danger to which they would be exposed, of contracting fever, and ague, in the swamps of the Rideau, I had provided myself with an ample supply of quinine, not one case occurred among them which required a single dose of this, or any other medicine, since we left Montreal.

Brydone, *Narrative*

The next day they reached Toronto, 273 km further on. As soon as they arrived Mr Brydone called on the government agent for emigrants, a Mr A. B. Hawke.

. . . He accompanied me to the governor's house, where I was graciously received, delivered my credentials and was directed by His Excellency, Sir John Colborne, to allow as many of the people as could find

FAR LEFT: Emigrants finally setting sail. Overcrowding on the ships was very common, so any disease spread quickly. Some emigrants failed to reach their destination
LEFT: Because the journey took many weeks, the emigrants stayed on deck whenever possible. The first sight of land came as a great relief
BELOW: All emigrants had to have a medical inspection

employment for themselves to do so. An open shed on the beach, or bay, was allotted for the people generally; a small house, at a considerable distance, with two or three rooms, was provided for one or two families, West's particularly, whose wife expected daily her confinement.

All however declined accommodation provided for them, and found lodgings for themselves; the heavy luggage I deposited in a store on the wharf.

Brydone, *Narrative*

Since the next day was Sunday Mr Brydone went to some trouble to find food for his party. He then 'called on Mr Jones of the Canada Company and found a letter from the Rev. T. Sockett. A most agreeable and delightful circumstance, to receive intelligence of friends at a distance'. Mr Sockett instructed him to return by a different route, in order to find out which would be better for future emigrants. He told him to:

. . . Return by New York, and communicate with our English Emigration agents, at every station, explaining your commission from us, and reason for so doing. Some plan might possibly be hit upon for parties to be met at Toronto; Hamilton; Fort George; Niagara; or the Welland canal: we shall not complain of any expense which tends to the main object; relief on this side; improvement on that.

I am above all things anxious that you should return fully informed upon every point; and furnished with every book; map; plan; every document of every kind, that for love or money, you can lay your hand upon.

Brydone, *Narrative*

But before he returned there were still one or two things to see to in Toronto:

**June 17th.** Accompanied by Mr Hawke, I waited on the Governor, who received me in the most affable manner. His Excellency directed that all the families should proceed to Blandford; where he was certain they would find employment; that each family should receive a five acre lot of cleared land in the township, on which a log hut should be erected; that they should hold the above for a few years, or until they could do better for themselves.

That such of the young men as I thought fit, and were willing, should go to the canal forming on the Grand River, or to the harbour at Kettle Creek, where they would find employment, at from £2 to £3 per month: and that the others should accompany the families to Blandford, where several gentlemen had lately made purchases of lands; and where labourers were much required.

Brydone, *Narrative*

Mr Brydone explored the area around Toronto as thoroughly as he could. On one of his expeditions to a slightly more remote area he met a mill owner, a Mr Cushing, who was able to give him a Canadian view of Sussex emigrants:

I told him that I had just brought out 135 emigrants from Sussex. He asked me if they were Lord Egremont's people; and on my saying they were, he remarked: that Lord Egremont had sent out a party for the last three years: that they were generally considered in the country as a superior class of labourers; and he wished some of them would come his way; but added he was too far in the bush to expect that.

Brydone, *Narrative*

Mr Brydone regarded his travels as a kind of investigation. Wherever he went he noticed things which he thought would be useful to future emigrants, and asked questions of the people he met: how much did land cost? Would new settlers need to clear it themselves? How fertile was the soil? What kind of workers were most needed?

Before he began the return journey all his party of emigrants had moved from the barns where they had first stayed into permanent homes. He remarked:

. . . I was thus enabled, with peculiar satisfaction to myself, to leave these people, in

RIGHT: The newly arrived immigrants could expect plenty of hard work if they were to make a success of the decision to emigrate

*On the Road*

*Crossing a River*

*The Second Season*

*The First Season*

whose welfare I had taken a deep interest, and for whom I had felt a considerable degree of anxiety, contented and happy, in the prospect now opened to them, of present comfort, and ultimate independence.
Brydone, *Narrative*

There was the prospect too of employment and homes for future emigrants, as Mr Brydone reported:

I had an audience of His Excellency, in which I reported to him, the very comfortable state I found our emigrants in, on my return to them, at the end of a month after their location, that all were in full employment, contented and happy.

His Excellency was much pleased to hear so favourable a report, and said that although he could not give the same assistance to all, who came out, he would still do everything in his power, particularly for large families. That he had represented to the Secretary for the Colonies, that he could receive 100 000 emigrants annually; that he would find employment for all who came out; that it was part of his plan to set them to work in cutting down the timber, and clearing the land, not in such a way as would enable them to make high wages; but at the usual rate paid in the colony for such labour; and so as to provide them with the means of subsistence, until they could do better for themselves: that the purchasers of land would

repay this expence; and that it would be to the advantage of them to do so, in order to possess a portion ready cleared, the moment of their arrival, at as low a rate as they themselves could effect it: but that ultimately the labourers must depend on their own exertions.

Brydone, *Narrative*

ABOVE: A shanty in the Bush

## The emigrants abroad

Mr Brydone looked on his venture as a great success, but what did members of the emigration party feel?

Of those who chose to emigrate, few can have foreseen the consequences of their decision. One whose dreams appeared to have come true was William Green, who travelled with the party from Petworth on the *British Tar* in 1834. He wrote:

### SOURCE 102 An emigrant's view of his new life

. . . Relating to myself and family we are all well: and doing very well just now; have got my order for 200 acres of land, which I intend to go to in spring. People may say what they will concerning America, it is one of the finest countries, for a poor man that is industrious, for he has to want for nothing . . .

Rev. T. Sockett (ed), *Continuation of Letters from Sussex Emigrants*, 1832

Generally, letters tell us that the emigrants were fairly happy in Canada. If they worked hard they could soon raise enough money to buy land and build themselves a house.

George Sullington, a labourer from Sullington, Sussex, went out with one of the first parties from Petworth in 1832. His letter is typical of many others:

### SOURCE 103 Another emigrant reassures his parents

Dear Father and Mother,

. . . I like the country here very much, but my wife don't seem to quite so well contented yet. I got work the first day I was here, and have had plenty of work ever since. I got six shillings per day (New York currency) which is 3s 9d English money, and be boarded. Farmers and labourers all sit at one table here. I don't wish to persuade anyone to come over, for they must expect to see a good many hardships; but I know that a poor man can do a great deal better here than he can at home: he is sure to get plenty of work, if he is steady, and can live cheaper. I have bought a cow for £5, and a young sow for 12s 6d. We work here from sun-rise to sun-set; but we don't work so hard as we do at home . . . Dear Father and Mother, we left you almost broken hearted, but you must be satisfied that we have bettered our condition by coming here . . .

Rev. T. Sockett (ed), *Letters from Sussex Emigrants*, 1832

Mr Brydone's account of the journey to Toronto and his explorations while he was there reflect the complex problems and decisions involved in emigrating to another country. You must take into account that Mr Brydone's account of the journey was written for his employers, but even allowing for this, the journey seems to have been a remarkably smooth one by the standards of the day. You may think that the emigrants had everything done for them once they had taken the decision to join the party, but when you look more closely you will see that this is not so. For instance, no-one could decide for them what to do once the party reached its destination. In any case you will find Mr Brydone having to take all kinds of decisions which on most voyages would be left to individuals.

Why did these people from Petworth decide to emigrate? We can't be certain because we don't know anything about them as individuals, other than what we are told in Mr Brydone's account of the voyage. But we can imagine them, and other emigrants from Petworth, deliberating over the kind of information which the Emigration Committee was able to provide about the journey, the kinds of workers needed in Upper Canada, and the land available. As for why they chose to go to Toronto and the area around, in a sense this was an obvious choice for them to make. If they had decided to go elsewhere, they would have had to make all their own arrangements, probably travel to a more distant port before starting their voyage, and take all kinds of risks, from which the local committee protected them.

Few early nineteenth century emigrants can have known as much about what was in store for them as those from Petworth.

ABOVE: An emigrant's dream. It did come true for some people

# 3
# The Church and Social Reform

## Social conditions

Between 1801 and 1851 the population increased by ten million. Attracted by wages offered in manufacturing work, many people moved to the rapidly growing towns and cities. This migration added to urban populations which were already increasing due to the changes in both the birth and death rates (source 104).

We have already seen in the section on 'The Vote', that this process presented problems for the country's system of government. But it also caused social problems, some of which we are still living with today.

People were crowded into small, insanitary dwellings, and many had no home at all. Bad housing and a poor diet led to illness, a major cause of long-term poverty. Manufacturing workers were entirely dependent on the state of trade.

As we saw in the section on 'The Poor', a trade depression or illness would result in dire hardship (sources 105, 106).

Employers got their money's worth—and more. This was especially true in the case of child labour. Employers had an interest in avoiding factory accidents but beyond that, contemporary reports and pamphlets show that in many cases children were treated very badly (sources 107, 108).

Urban living conditions offered numerous opportunities for crime. Many people resorted to crime from desperation in times of difficulty. Once convicted, a petty thief, for example, might be transported to Australia, or serve a sentence in a filthy, over-crowded prison.

OPPOSITE: An early photograph of working class housing in Wolverhampton

Janet Cumming, eleven years old, bears coals, and says:
" I gang with the women at five and come up at five at night; work *all night* on Fridays, and come away at twelve in the day. I carry the large bits of coal from the wall-face to the pit-bottom, and the small pieces, called chows, in a creel. The weight is usually a hundred-weight; does not know how many pounds there are in a hundred-weight, but it is some weight to carry; it takes three journeys to fill a tub of four hundred-weight. The distance varies, as the work is not always on the same wall; sometimes 150 fathoms, whiles 250 fathoms. The roof is very low; I have to bend my back and legs, and the water comes frequently up to the calves of my legs. Has no liking for the work; father makes me like it. Never got hurt, but often obliged to scramble out of the pit when bad air was in." (Ibid., p. 436.)

The following represents an older girl carrying coals.

Isabella Read, twelve years old:
" I am wrought with sister and brother; it is very sore work. Cannot say how many rakes, or journeys, I make from pit-bottom to wall-face and back, thinks about thirty or twenty-five on the average; distance varies from 100 to 250 fathoms. I carry a hundred-weight and a quarter on my back, and am frequently in water up to the calves of my legs. When first down, fell frequently asleep while waiting for coal, from heat and fatigue. I do not like the work, nor do the lassies, but they are made to like it. When the weather is warm, there is difficulty in breathing, and frequently the lights go out." (Ibid., p. 439.)
Agnes Kerr, fifteen years old, coal-bearer, Dryden Colliery:
" Was nine years old when commenced carrying coals; carry father's coal; make eighteen to twenty journeys a-day; a journey to and fro is about 200 to 250 fathoms; have to ascend and descend many ladders; can carry 1¼ cwt." (Ibid., p. 448.)

ABOVE: A page from the 1842 Mines Report describes child labour in the coal mines. This Report had great impact because it was illustrated. As a result of the Report to Parliament, children under ten and women were not allowed to work underground

## SOURCE 104 **The growth of towns**

. . . By reference to the Population Returns it appears that, from the beginning of the present century, the whole population of Great Britain has increased at the rate of nearly 16 per cent every ten years . . . Whilst the increase of population in England and Wales from 1801 to 1831, has been something more than 47 per cent, the actual increase in the number of inhabitants of five of our most important provincial towns has very nearly doubled that rate; being Manchester 109 per cent, Glasgow 108 per cent, Birmingham 73 per cent, Leeds 99 per cent, Liverpool 100 per cent.

*Report of the Select Committee on the Health of Towns*, Parliamentary Papers, 1840, Vol. XI, p. iv

RIGHT: A *Punch* cartoon points out the link between overcrowding, bad sanitation and epidemic disease

## SOURCE 105 Scottish colliers' homes

. . . The roof is frequently insufficient, admitting wind and rain in wet and windy weather . . . In some the rafters and thatch are quite rotten and decayed . . . In the worst kind of these houses the apartment is ill supplied with light, the windows being only partially supplied with glass, and its place supplied with paper, bundles of rags, and old hats. In some of these houses the windows cannot be opened . . .

The floors of the cottages inhabited by colliers are composed generally of beaten earth. These floors are very dirty, and so uneven as to make a stranger almost fall. It is not uncommon to see holes and depressions in these floors formed in the course of time by various causes . . . The bedstead is generally covered with dust, and with innumerable flymarks. In summer, bugs in multitudes may be seen, more especially at night, when the light of a candle is suddenly thrown upon the bedstead. The odour of these apartments is most offensive and sickening, from the long-continued presence of human impurities.

R. Scott Alison, M.D., 'Report on the sanitary conditions of . . . Tranent, and neighbouring district at Haddingtonshire', Parliamentary Papers, Lords, 1842, Vol. XXVII, quoted in E. Royston Pike, *Human Documents of the Industrial Revolution*, Allen & Unwin, 1970, pp. 329-30

## SOURCE 106 Sanitation, illness and poverty

Sewerage, drainage, and cleansing is (in many places inhabited by dense masses of the working classes) greatly neglected; . . . the most necessary precautions to preserve their health in many cases appears to have been forgotten; . . . in consequence, fevers and other disorders of a contagious and fatal nature are shown to prevail to a very alarming extent, causing widespread misery among the families of the sufferers, often entailing weakness and prostration of strength among the survivors; and becoming the source of great expense to the parishes and more opulent classes . . .

*Report of the Select Committee on the Health of Towns*, Parliamentary Papers, 1840, Vol. XI, p. 7

## SOURCE 107 Factory accidents

. . . I learned that accidents were very rare, and that, when they did occur, they were, as my own senses convinced me that they must have been, the result of the grossest negligence or of absolute wilfulness. I mention this circumstance because the burst of

G

sentimental sympathy for the condition of the factory-operatives . . . appealed largely to the number of accidents which happened from machinery, and I was myself for a time fool enough to believe that mills were places in which young children were, by some inexplicable process, ground-bones, flesh, and blood together—into yarn and printed calicoes. I remember very well when first I visited a cotton-mill feeling something like disappointment at not discovering the hoppers into which the infants were thrown. I have since found that such absurdity is only credited by those who, like myself at that period, could not tell the difference between a cotton-mill and a tread-mill. But a very little consideration should have taught me better; derangements of machinery are very expensive accidents to remedy; and if the mill-owners of Lanca-shire were as reckless of human life as the worst of their assailants have chosen to describe them, they certainly are not men likely to disregard their own pockets. I have had some opportunities of estimating the cost of accidents, and I know that the engi-neers' bill is considerably heavier than the surgeon's.

Taylor, *Notes of a Tour of the Manufacturing Districts of Lancashire*, p. 25

## SOURCE 108 A factory apprentice

Once in ten days, or a fortnight, the whole of the finer machinery used to be taken to pieces and cleaned, and then they had to remain at the mill from morning till night, and frequently have been unable to find time to get any food from this early breakfast till night, . . . a term frequently extended from fifteen to sixteen hours incessant labour.

As an inducement to the children to volunteer to work the whole dinner-hour, a premium of a halfpenny was allowed! Small as was the bribe, it induced many, and Blincoe amongst the number! On such occasions, the dinner was brought up in tin cans, and often has Blincoe's allowance stood till night, whilst he was almost famished with hunger, and he has often carried it back, or rather eaten it on the road, cold, nauseous, and covered with flue [cotton fluff].

John Brown, *A Memoir of Robert Blincoe*, 1832, p. 22

LEFT: Children worked in all branches of industry, not just in mines and textile factories. This picture shows a brick works where children were employed to carry clay and the finished bricks. Hours of work and discipline were as long and severe as in factories, and a child might walk up to 16 kilometres during a day's work; most of it in the open air

## Whose responsibility?

Nowadays, we would say that it was up to the Government to improve social conditions. In the long run the Government did bring about improvements in the nineteenth century, but it was a slow process. Many people thought that it was wrong for Parliament to interfere with people's freedom—the freedom, for example, of a mill owner to run his factory as he pleased (source 109).

### SOURCE 109 Why factories should not be regulated

If the Manufacturers of this country be fairly treated, they will go on increasing . . . assured employment and diminishing the cost of the articles they make, to the benefit of all persons of every rank, but more especially the poorer members of the state. If they be vilified and fettered as ignorant meddling enthusiasts and philanthropists are now attempting, but not at their own expense, establishments for spinning and weaving will still flourish,—but not in Great Britain.

Joseph Birley, *Sadler's Bill*, 1832, p. 7

Other people like Samuel Smiles ('The Poor,' source 54), would have claimed that difficulties should be met by self-help. Yet when working people tried to help themselves through, say, political organisations, they met strong opposition. ('The Vote'.) Yet there was another agency which might have helped : the churches.

This section examines the contribution made by the churches to social reform during the period we are studying. First, though, we must look at the way people regarded the churches at this time.

BELOW: A cartoon shows how profits are made. In the shop, a lady is saying, 'I cannot imagine how they can possibly be made for the price'

# The church and the people

### 'The multitude we see not'

The Church of Scotland already carried the chief responsibility for looking after the poor in Scotland. In other areas, parish churches, dissenting chapels, Roman Catholic chapels—none were equipped to cope with the sudden growth of population in towns and cities. In addition, many churchmen were not particularly concerned with the sort of people who faced the kind of problems mentioned in previous pages. On the whole, churches were for the middle classes (sources 110-112), although some contemporaries recognised that this gap between church and people in need existed (source 113).

### Attitudes

What were the reasons for this lack of contact between the churches and 'the multitude we see not'?

One reason was that respectability was considered a virtue. The diseased, the uneducated, and poor were not respectable (sources 114, 115). More important were the attitudes and examples offered by many churchmen (sources 116-120).

Where there was contact, the churches often seemed to ignore the possibility of improving society. All too often they seemed to suggest that hardship was inevitable for some, and that it should be borne patiently and obediently (source 121).

In these circumstances, the churches became another example of the way society was divided. For the new class of town workers in particular, the church was on the 'other side' (source 122).

## SOURCE 110 Numbers of worshippers, 1851

### TABLE 1

| | |
|---|---|
| Total population of England & Wales | 17 927 609 |
| No. of possible worshippers | 12 549 326 |

(This estimates that 30 per cent of the population were unable to attend church once on Sunday and includes young children, old people, invalids and Sunday workers.)

| | |
|---|---|
| No. of actual worshippers | 7 261 032 |
| (This includes) | |
| Church of England | 3 773 474 |
| Scottish Presbyterians | 60 131 |
| Independents | 793 142 |
| Baptists | 587 978 |
| Quakers | 18 172 |
| Wesleyan Methodists | 1 385 382 |
| Welsh Calvinistic Methodists | 151 046 |
| Roman Catholics | 305 393 |
| Mormons | 18 800 |
| Jews | 4 150 |

Extract from an official (1854) report by Horace Mann based on the *Census of Great Britain, 1851— Religious worship in England and Wales*

## SOURCE 111 Middle class Christianity

The census results hammered home what had already become clear to many ministers and concerned laymen, namely, that the churches by and large were basically middle

ABOVE: Down and outs seek admittance to a night refuge. Lord Shaftesbury calculated that London possessed 30 000 homeless children alone, apart from adults like those shown here

class institutions. 'British Christianity', declared Edward Miall in the *Nonconformist* in 1849, 'is essentially the Christianity developed by a middle class soil.'

J. F. C. Harrison, *The Early Victorians, 1832-51*, Weidenfeld and Nicolson, 1968, pp. 123-4

### SOURCE 112 **Horace Mann's conclusions**

The most important fact which this investigation as to attendance brings before us is, unquestionably, the alarming number of the non-attendants. Even in the least unfavourable aspect of the figures just presented, and assuming (as no doubt is right) that the 5 288 294 absent every Sunday are not always the same individuals, it must be apparent that a sadly formidable portion of the English people are habitual neglectors of the public ordinances of religion. Nor is it difficult to indicate to what particular class of the community this portion in the main belongs . . . While the labouring myriads of our country have been multiplying with our multiplied material prosperity, it cannot, it is feared, be stated that a corresponding increase has occurred in the attendance of this class in our religious edifices. More especially in cities and large towns it is observable how absolutely insignificant a portion of the congregations is composed of artisans. They fill, perhaps, in youth our National, British, and Sunday-Schools, and there receive the elements of a religious education: but no sooner do they mingle in the active world of labour, than, subjected to the constant action of opposing influences, they soon become as utter strangers to religious ordinances as the people of a heathen country. From whatever cause, in them or in the manner of their treatment by religious bodies, it is sadly certain that this vast, intelligent, and growingly important section of our country-men is thoroughly estranged from our religious institutions in their present aspect.

*Religious Worship in England and Wales*

### SOURCE 113 **Samuel Wilberforce, a son of William Wilberforce who later became Bishop of Oxford, draws attention to the problem of non-attenders at church**

We look, it may be, every Sunday, at our well-filled churches, and we forget, for the moment, in the presence of those we see, the multitude we see not; the mass behind; whom misery, as well as sin, whom want of room, want of clothes, indolence, neglect or utter wretchedness, are shutting out from our fellowship, and severing from civilisation

BELOW: Samuel Wilberforce. Son of the famous slave trade abolitionist, he was Bishop of Oxford 1845-69. The efficiency of his administration served as a model for other dioceses

and religion. Yet there they surely are. In all our great towns thin walls separate luxury from starvation. The two classes live in absolute ignorance of each other; the two streams nowhere intermingle: selfish respectability degrades one set; whilst misery and recklessness, which soon turn into vice and wickedness, weigh down the other.

Samuel Wilberforce, *A Charge delivered to the Clergy of the Archdeaconry of Surrey*, London, 1844, pp. 15-16

## SOURCE 114 Respectability

Those who are in this state [poverty] are naturally reluctant to mingle themselves with the richer: they are unwilling to exhibit poverty and rags in contrast with wealth or splendour. The very act of attending the house of God requires in them something of an effort; and they are moreover continually and importunately tempted to withdraw themselves . . .

J. B. Sumner, *A Charge delivered to the Clergy of the Diocese of Chester*, Hatchard, 1838, p. 12

## SOURCE 115 Reasons for middle class attendance

The middle classes of England are most distinguished for church-going habits. It is one of their traditional properties to be associated with some place of worship. But there are not wanting indications that many come into all our churches who would not be found there, were they less influenced by the respectabilities; that many are there rather from habit and regard for appearances, than from real respect for Christ's ordinance of social worship and real desire for Christian edification.

A. Mackennal in A. P. Stanley *et al.*, *Sermons Preached to Working People*, Macmillan, 1867, p. 90

## SOURCE 116 Rich and poor

God never meant that the idle should live upon the labour of the industrious . . . He hath therefore permitted a state of property to be everywhere introduced; that the industrious might enjoy the rewards of their diligence; and that those who would not work, might feel the punishment of their laziness.

From a sermon by Richard Watson, Bishop of Llandaff; in R. A. Solway, *Prelates and People, 1783-1852*, Routledge & Kegan Paul, 1968, p. 78

BELOW: Churchgoing was for the middle classes. A vicar greets his congregation at Christmas

### SOURCE 117 Attitudes to hardship

A preacher could spend his life surrounded by the squalor of a manufacturing town without feeling any twinge of socially radical sentiment, when he believed that many poor people were suffering for their own sins, and that the plight of the rest was the result of spiritual ordinances which it would be impious to question and of economic laws, which it would be foolish to resist; charity could alleviate the suffering caused by these laws, but in any case the poor had only to wait until death for the end of all temporal hardships and distinctions. Many men who believed these things were humane . . .

K. S. Inglis, *Churches and the Working Classes in Victorian England*, Routledge & Kegan Paul, 1969, p. 251

### SOURCE 118 Divisions in church

Some of the pews for the rich were padded, lined, cushioned, and supplied with every comfort . . . The poor, on the other hand, were seated on stools in the aisles; many of the seats were without backs, to prevent the occupants from falling asleep during the sermon, and the cold, damp stone beneath their feet, was the only place to kneel during prayer . . . Some of our Church ministers of that day appeared to have fellowship only with the wealthy.

John Glyde, *The Moral, Social and Religious Condition of Ipswich 1850*, S R Publishers, 1971 edition, p. 225

### SOURCE 119 Another view of the poor

For these things does my heart fail within me when I see in the poor, no marks of deference to the rich, in the ignorant none of submission to the wise, in the labourer none of attachment to his employer:—when I hear no more . . . the sound of the shuttle in the cottage, nor the merry carol in the fields; when I see boys lured to sin through the cheapness of intemperance, and girls growing up to womanhood in ignorance of the simplest household cares; when I am told in a whisper, of depravities of which Pauperism is the parent.

Rev T. Thorp, *Individual Vice, Social Sin*, 1832, p. 14

## SOURCE 120 Working to rule

In the parish of St Lawrence, the sum of £40 was annually subscribed by the performance of an afternoon service; . . . and when from deaths and removals, the subscriptions
fell short of that amount, the minister declined to perform the duty unless the usual
sum was collected.
Glyde, *Condition of Ipswich*, 1850, p. 225

## SOURCE 121 Church education

In the school and the church, the people are taught that passive obedience is a virtue—
that faith is paramount to knowledge, and that the fear of hell is more salutory for the
poor man's soul, than to confide in the mercy of God . . . They are taught to believe
that they are mercifully created to endure poverty, and that the rich are very unfortunate in being born to the care and trouble of ruling over the poor. They are also
taught, that God has created them poor, for the salvation of their immortal souls; and
that through tribulation they must enter Heaven. They are taught that to fret at their
earthly privations, is to rebel against the goodness of God, and for which, they must
incur his everlasting displeasure . . .
*Chartist Circular*, 30 November 1839

## SOURCE 122 Church and class—a churchman's view

The people in agricultural districts are generally indifferent about the Church—luke
warmness is their sin; the upper and middle classes uphold her;—but in the manufacturing districts she is the object of detestation to the working classes. Among this class I
have many friends, zealous and enlightened Churchmen; and from them, and the
persecutions they endure, I know the feeling which exists. The working classes consider
themselves to be an oppressed people . . . they consider the Church to belong to the
Party of the their oppressors; hence they hate it, and consider a man of the working-
classes who is a Churchman to be a traitor to his Party or Order—he is outlawed in the
society in which he moves. Paupers and persons in need may go to church on the
principle of living on the enemy; but woe to the young man in health and strength who
proclaims himself a Churchman.
Part of a letter from Dr Walter Farquhar Hook, Vicar of Leeds, to Archdeacon Samuel Wilberforce,
5 July 1843; in A. R. Ashwell, *Life of the Right Reverend Samuel Wilberforce*, London, 1880–82, Vol. I, p. 225

ABOVE: Churchgoing in the 1830s

# The church and social problems

The previous section shows relations between the churches and the general population at their worst. It is true that some church people did think in a negative way: even epidemics like the cholera outbreak in 1848 were seen by some as God's judgement rather than the result of weaknesses in city government (source 123).

Yet, during the period we are studying, there are some signs that the churches generally as well as individual Christian philanthropists became more involved in reform movements, even though their motives were sometimes questionable (source 124).

RIGHT: A sweeping measure. This cartoon comments on policies for homeless children; many found themselves emigrating. Significantly (to the cartoonist) a vicar is helping to clear up the children. He is saying, 'According to the teachings of Jesus, all these little gutter girls are our sisters, and therefore I feel it my duty as a Christian Minister to assist in this good work'

## SOURCE 123 God's judgement

Whatever may be the opinion formed respecting the nature and the causes of the fearful disease which is now sweeping away such multitudes of persons, in all ranks of society; there can be no doubt . . . that God is using it as the rod of his indignation to chastise us for our iniquities, and to bring us to sincere and genuine repentance.

Rev John King, *The Cholera, God's Sore Judgement on the Nations of the Earth*, 1849, p. 2

## SOURCE 124 A motive for reform

The love of our country also and of social order, no less than the feelings of humanity demand of us an unlimited liberality. Wild doctrines are abroad; advantage has been taken of distress to excite the worst passions of the sufferers; there is no arguing with a famished man.

Thorp, *Individual Vice, Social Sin*, p. 13

### Methodists

One of the main reasons for this growing involvement was the way Methodism revived in the nineteenth century and identified itself with the poorer people in society (source 125). John Glyde described its effects on Ipswich (source 126).

In many areas, there was another side to the link between Methodism and the working classes—political involvement (source 127).

ABOVE: At times of general hardship, the local church might organise relief. In this picture, Coventry weavers are being given soup in the kitchen at St Mary's Hall

## SOURCE 125 Methodism in the North-East

The colliers of Northumberland and Durham are a century in advance of their class in any other mining district in England, Scotland or Wales . . .

The owners had early seen the capability of the organisation and labours of the Methodists being especially adapted to improve the population; for the colliery people were collected in places mostly lying apart from the established parish churches, which then had no curates or scripture readers going forth to reach such people. The owners wisely facilitated the operations of the Wesleyans in opening Sunday schools and chapels. Many of the colliers became local preachers, and promoted the mental culture of their own class.

R. Lowery, in *The Weekly Record*, 14 June 1856

ABOVE: A Methodist preaching in the open

## SOURCE 126 John Glyde describes the effects of the revival

It was not the Establishment [Church of England] merely that made known the fact, that the spirit of Christ had but little manifestation in his church. Nonconformists were apathetic: ... Wesleyanism was feeble, having but just commenced its noble mission to the poor. Sunday was invariably a day of pleasure; and amusements, not of a very innocent character, were freely indulged in. It was quite a chance if some one was not placed in the stocks; and it was the best day in the week for the publican. When the shades of evening came over, tradesmen were frequently seen reeling to their homes. A few years later, and this awful state of things had begun to pass away. The disciples of John Wesley gained a footing, and threw open the doors of Christ's kingdom to all. They moved among the poor; and, by their earnestness and self sacrifice, gained the love and reverence of the care-worn and the prostrate. The extent and nature of Wesleyan influence among the neglected classes were soon manifest, and not the least of the benefits it conferred, was the partial awakening of the members of other churches to a sense of their neglect in reference to their poor brethren. The very fact of the people flocking eagerly to hear the stirring appeals of the disciples of Wesley, is conclusive that the Establishment, and other religious bodies in the town at that period, failed in supplying the religious wants of the masses.

Glyde, *Condition of Ipswich, 1850*

## SOURCE 127 Impact of the Methodists

The Methodists ... brought great powers of leadership to the working-class political societies and trade unions. Joseph Capper, the Primitive Methodist Chartist leader of the Potteries, had 'a tongue like the sledgehammer he used in his shop'. Tommy Hepburn, the Primitive Methodist leader of the Durham miners, 'could be heard at one time by forty thousand people, and always carried the multitude with him'. One coal-owner told a Royal Commission that 'the men professing to be Methodists and Ranters [Primitive Methodists] are the spokesmen on these occasions, and the most difficult to deal with. These men may be superior men to the rest in intelligence, and generally show great skill, and cunning, and circumvention'. H. S. Tremenheere, the Inspector of Mines, wrote of prayer meetings of striking colliers in 1844, where local preachers, 'by certain command of language and energetic tone and manner, had acquired an influence over their fellow workmen and were invariably the chief promoters and abettors of the strikes'.

H. Perkin, *The Origins of Modern English Society 1780–1880*, Routledge & Kegan Paul, 1969, p. 357

## Evangelicals

As John Glyde suggested, other churches were influenced by the Methodists. In the Church of England the most active group was known as the Evangelicals. They had no time for outward appearances, believing that faith in God made a pauper as near to heaven as a bishop.

Their attitude to the working classes and the poor was similar to that of the Methodists, and movements like the Christian Socialist Movement which had close links with the Evangelicals did much to widen the appeal of Christianity (sources 128-131).

### SOURCE 128 Advances for the Evangelicals

Evangelical religion is, we contend, the chief cause of the improvement so manifest in the great masses of English society. We do not mean that great numbers are converted to God, but we do mean that great numbers are, more or less (and now, far more than ever), under the indirect influence of the Christian religion.

*Congregational Year Book, 1849*, p. 76

### SOURCE 129 Impact of the Christian Socialist Movement, 1860: Letter from W. F. Hook, Vicar of Leeds to F. D. Maurice, one of the leaders of the Christian Socialist Movement

The great good done by yourself and Co., is this, that the working classes have learned to consider Christians and Churchmen, what they are, their friends. I lived for thirty-three years among them in Birmingham, Coventry and Leeds. Three and thirty years ago we were regarded with hatred. It is very different now—at least in Yorkshire. The step our generation has made is this. The working classes respect Christianity though they stand aloof and only a few of them come to Church, but they readily hand over to us the next generation for education.

Perkin, *Origins of Modern English Society*, p. 364

ABOVE: Frederick Denison Maurice. He sympathised with much of the Chartist programme and hoped to win over some of its former supporters to a reformed church

## SOURCE 130 A change in attitude

Every denomination of religion is more active in its operations to do good since then, and especially the Church of England clergy. The mere fox-hunting, sporting and jolly-living parson who entered the church for the living has almost died out, and a new race of earnest men devoted to the duties of their office have sprung up. Twenty years ago when moving about I found a general disrespect for the parsons, as they were called. The word was used to express contempt and condemnation, as of one who drew the salary and did not fulfil the duties of an office . . . Now the churches are extended, the clergy and the curates generally respected, and active in instructing the poor.

R. Lowery, in *The Weekly Record*, 2 August 1856

## SOURCE 131 Aims of the Christian Socialist Movement

The Church's mission was to be 'the leader of all privations, and diseases, the bond of all classes, the instrument for reforming abuses, the admonisher of the rich, the friend of the poor, the asserter of the glory of that humanity which Christ bears'.

C. F. G. Masterman, *Frederick Denison Maurice*, London & Oxford, 1907, p. 234; in Inglis, *Churches and the Working Classes in Victorian England*, p. 272

BELOW: Down and outs in a London night refuge, listening to a Bible reading before lights-out
BELOW RIGHT: A Mission for seamen. These were supported by the churches and often provided accommodation and some social services

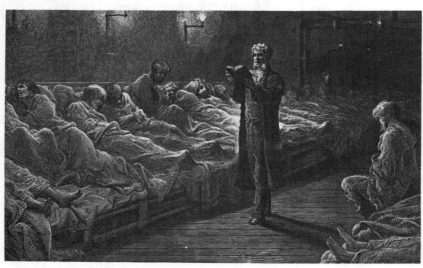

# Individuals

It is becoming clear now that it is hard to make a generalisation about the Church and social reform. We have seen that there was much that was wrong with the way the churches acted. But we must also take into account the good work of individual Christians.

The majority, like the vicar of Aberford in Yorkshire, who paid the village school bills from his own pocket, or James Begg, the Scottish Free Church minister who worked hard to improve working class housing, have not become world famous. Others, like the Evangelical Lord Shaftesbury, have become internationally known for devoting their lives to charitable work (sources 132, 133).

ABOVE: Lord Shaftesbury

### SOURCE 132  Local charity
### Aberford, 4th January 1871

The Vicar ventures to ask the attention of a few of his parishioners to the following statement.

The question now comes before us whether we shall have a school supported by voluntary contributions or a school supported by Rates. The advantages of the present system are that we may teach Christian doctrine in the school freely . . . In a Rate supported school on the contrary, no creed or catechism can be introduced . . . But the Rate supported school has this attraction, that they release the Incumbent of the parish from pecuniary responsibility; he pays his Rate and then is free.

In this parish it has fallen to the Vicar to make up from his own means each year, deficits in the accounts which joined to an equal sum for expenses which could not be avoided (school prizes are yearly entertainment of children) has required from him an outlay of more than £500.

This scale of outlay the Vicar is not able to continue and he believes the parishioners would not desire it of him.
Printed Circular, private papers

### SOURCE 133  Shaftesbury's motivation
### December 17, 1827

First, I must now choose my line of life, and stand to it manfully. After some thought, I see nothing but a political career, for every one must take that in which his various circumstances will give him the best means of doing good. Where can I be so useful

ABOVE: Shaftesbury's interest in education was directed towards the 'ragged schools'. This picture shows the Ragged School Union annual prize giving

as in the public service? This question could be easily answered did it require but zeal, patriotism, honesty; but there is likewise a need of talent and knowledge. Yet, perhaps my success in earlier life has made me a debtor, and I am bound to try what God has put into me for the benefit of old England! . . . and having throughout desired nothing but this glory and the consummation of His word, conclude in the same, to the advancement of religion and the increase of human happiness.

*Shaftesbury's Diary*, in E. Hodder, *The Life and Work of . . . Shaftesbury*, London, 1887, pp. 43-4

## Elizabeth Fry and prison reform

Elizabeth Fry is another example of a person who wanted to spread Christianity through helping others. She devoted most of her life to prison reform. When she died in 1845, the *Illustrated London News* published her obituary:

### SOURCE 134 Elizabeth Fry's work recognised

Her whole life was one continued course of active exertion, which has been attended with many beneficial results. She gave much attention to the condition of female convicts and prisoners, at a time when our prison discipline and management were many degrees worse than they are now. Her efforts secured her the respect of all Christians, and acquired for her name European reputation.

*Illustrated London News*, 1845

## Elizabeth Fry's background

The Society of Friends (Quakers) provided Elizabeth Fry's religious background. Her father, a Norwich banker called John Gurney, did not believe in strict religious discipline, but when Elizabeth was eighteen years old, her sister Catherine noticed a change in her (source 135).

Reluctantly, in 1800, Elizabeth married a London banker called Joseph Fry. She bore him ten children over the next sixteen years, but at the same time as she was making a home and family, the feeling grew in her that she must express her religion in some practical way.

## Newgate

In 1817, Elizabeth Fry accompanied a friend on a visit to Newgate prison. Conditions were wretched, particularly for the women and children prisoners.

'It was', she wrote afterwards, 'more like a slave ship. The begging, swearing, gaming, fighting, singing, dancing, dressing up in men's clothes were too bad to be described, so that we did not think it suitable to take a young person within'.

Two more visits followed, and then Elizabeth Fry threw herself wholeheartedly into the job of trying to improve conditions for the women prisoners. She organised a school for the children, she provided more clothes, she set up a ladies' association to investigate conditions and recommend improvements, and she persuaded both the Governor of

ABOVE: Women prisoners had their children with them. This picture shows exercise time in the Toothill Fields Prison, London

Newgate and the women prisoners to accept a set of rules for the better running of the prison.

Her main aim, however, was to bring the women prisoners into a better life through accepting Christ. Elizabeth Fry saw Christ as the purpose of all her work (sources 136-138).

## Journey to the north

Believing that the acceptance of her rules would improve other prisons, Elizabeth Fry now made a fact-finding journey with her brother, Joseph Gurney, to the north of England and Scotland (source 139).

Conditions were bad, especially in Scotland, but as well as commenting on physical conditions, Joseph Gurney always noted the opportunities in prisons for religious instruction (sources 140, 141).

## Importance of Elizabeth Fry

Elizabeth Fry spent the rest of her life travelling, discussing, writing—all for prison reform. She also became interested in other ways of bringing the knowledge of Christianity to people. However, her main achievement was the improvements at Newgate which influenced reforms elsewhere. Of that success she wrote in her Journal:

'I am ready to say, in the fulness of my heart, surely, "It is the Lord's doing, and marvellous in our eyes".'

RIGHT: A contemporary artist painted this picture of Elizabeth Fry working with women prisoners in Newgate Prison. The notice on the wall warns against defacing Bibles and prayer books

**SOURCE 135** **The change in Elizabeth Fry, noticed by her sister Catherine**

A change became daily more evident in her . . . When she told me she could not dance with us any more it was almost more than I could bear, and I tried to argue with her, and begged and persecuted her. But it was all in vain. The firmness of her character was now called into play and I never remember her to have been shaken in one single point which she felt to be her duty. The Bible became her study, visiting the poor, especially the sick, her great object.

G. King Lewis, *Elizabeth Fry*, 1910, p. 29

## SOURCE 136 The first visit to Newgate

They found about 300 women, with their numerous children, crowded together, without classification or employment of any kind, in the custody of one man and his son. They cooked, they washed and slept on the floor. When any stranger appeared they clamoured for money, with which, if given, they purchased liquors from a tap in the prison. The screaming and terrible language, the fighting and lawlessness were such that the Governor, we are told, never entered without great reluctance.

King Lewis, *Elizabeth Fry*, p. 47

## SOURCE 137 A visitor to the New Newgate

The court-yard, into which I was admitted instead of being peopled with beings scarcely human, blaspheming, fighting, tearing each other's hair or gaming with a filthy pack of cards for the very clothes they wore (which often did not suffice even for decency) presented a scene where stillness and prosperity reigned . . . At the head of a long table sat a lady belonging to the Society of Friends. She was reading aloud to about sixteen women prisoners, who were engaged in needle-work around it. Each wore a clean-looking blue apron and bib . . . They all rose on my entrance, courtsied respect-fully, and then at a signal given, resumed their seats and employments.

S. Corder, *Life of Elizabeth Fry*, Bennett, 1853, pp. 230-1

## SOURCE 138 Elizabeth Fry's dedication

Third Month, 7th [1817]

My mind and time have been much taken up with Newgate and its concerns . . . May I . . . be enabled to keep my eye singly unto the Lord, that what I do may be done heartily unto Him, and not, in any degree, unto man.

Elizabeth Fry, 'Journal,' in S. Corder, *Life of Elizabeth Fry*, p. 220-1

## SOURCE 139 Reasons for the survey of prisons

The principal object of our journey was connected with the concerns of our own religious society, that of Friends; but we also made a point of inspecting the prisons in the several towns, through which we passed . . . and I think it right to communicate to the public the information which we collected, in the hope that it may afford some fresh stimulus, to the zeal already prevalent for improving our system of prison discipline . . .

The better the actual state of our prisons is known and understood, the more clearly will all men see the necessity of these arrangements, by which there may be rendered schools of industry and virtue, instead of the very nurseries of crime.

Joseph Gurney, *Notes . . . on the Prisons in Scotland and the North of England*, Longman, 1819, iv-v

### SOURCE 140 Haddington County Jail

That part of the prison, which is allotted to criminals and vagrants consists of four cells on the ground floor, measuring respectively thirteen feet by eight, and one on the second story, measuring eleven feet by seven. It is difficult to conceive anything more

RIGHT: Elizabeth Fry felt that the way to keep people out of prison was to concentrate on reforming prisoners. Another view held at this time was that there would be fewer criminals if punishments were made more effective. This led to the building of new prisons like Pentonville where prisoners were to be kept separate at all times. This attempt to cut a man off from his evil companions led to the sort of exercise arrangements shown

entirely miserable than these cells. Very dark—excessively dirty—clay floors—no fire places—straw in one corner for a bed, with perhaps a single rug—a tub in each of them, the receptacle of all filth . . .

None of the prisoners were ironed, except one man who had attempted to break prison. This unfortunate person was fastened to a long iron bar. His legs, being passed through rings attached to the bar, were kept about two feet asunder, which resistance might be increased to three feet and a half at the pleasure of the jailor.

Gurney, *Prisons in Scotland and the North of England*, pp. 18-19

### SOURCE 141 Religion in prisons

Some of the prisons . . . for instance the Bridewells at Glasgow and Edinburgh, are regularly attended by a school-master. This arrangement affords to the ignorant of various ages, an opportunity of acquiring that scriptural knowledge, which may often be the means of turning them from darkness to light . . . In the great majority of these prisons, however, there is no provision of the kind; the weekly return of prayers and a sermon, is too often the only means of instruction afforded; and in many cases, even this is withheld.

Gurney, *Prisons in Scotland and the North of England*, pp. 126-7

LEFT: The same principles of punishment and isolation applied to oakum picking and the treadmill at Holloway

# 4
# Railways

## The beginning of railways

No one invented railways as we understand them. Wheeled trucks moving on rails had been used in Britain since the seventeenth century: and over a period of two hundred years various developments had occurred which led to the setting up of the first modern railway system in 1830

Wooden rails were replaced by cast-iron rails in the eighteenth century. At the beginning of the nineteenth century, engineers like Richard Trevithick, John Blenkinsop and William Hedley began to experiment with steam engines mounted on wheels and running on rails. In 1820, John Birkinshaw, a Northumberland iron worker, patented a method of rolling wrought iron rails which were stronger than those made from cast iron.

Trevithick did much of the pioneer work on locomotives. In 1804, he demonstrated with his experimental engine at Pennydarren that high pressure steam could be used to drive a locomotive. There was no explosion, as people had expected. By 1812, a railway engine was in regular commercial use at Middleton Colliery, Leeds. It drew coal trucks along a short length of line.

George Stephenson, a self-educated Northumberland engineer was also experimenting with locomotives at this time. He built his first locomotive, the *Blücher*, in 1814.

If Stephenson is remembered when other engineers are forgotten, it is because he was the man to foresee the importance of the locomotive and it was he who had the confidence and the ability to obtain backing for his schemes. He was helped in this by the growth in the early 1820s of propaganda in favour of railways (source 142).

ABOVE: As early as 1700, wagonways were in use in the North-East for transporting coal

OPPOSITE: Trevithick's experimental Racing Steam Horse on show in London in 1808

It was Stephenson who was responsible for the first mechanised railway financed by public money. It opened in 1825 and was built to carry coal between Darlington and the River Tees at Stockton (source 143).

The impact of this goods railway on the surrounding area was remarkable (source 144).

BELOW: The opening of the Stockton-Darlington Railway

ABOVE: George Stephenson

## The Liverpool – Manchester railway

The Stockton-Darlington railway had been built as an alternative to building a canal. In 1826, Parliament gave permission for a railway to be built between Liverpool and Manchester; this railway was meant to break the monopoly of an existing canal— the Bridgewater Canal. Accordingly, the project was much more controversial than the Stockton-Darlington, and a good deal of effort was spent on justifying the need for such a railway line (source 145).

George Stephenson was again chosen as engineer and had to bear the brunt of opposition from the canal company. Completing a survey of the line proved difficult (source 146).

When the line was discussed by a House of Commons committee, proceedings continued for 37 days, and the opposition tried to make Stephenson look a fool by questioning the accuracy of his survey and emphasising the difficulty of running a line across a notorious bog, Chat Moss (sources 147, 148).

Stephenson overcame this and other engineering problems, and the line was finished in four years.

Trials were held at Rainhill in 1829 to decide on the best form of traction. Robert Stephenson's *Rocket* was judged the best locomotive, and won for its builder a prize of £500. The line was opened eleven months later, in December 1830, though the opening ceremony was spoilt to some extent by a fatal accident to William Huskisson, MP for Liverpool.

The Liverpool-Manchester railway was the first wholly mechanised public railway, and it was an immediate success. Contemporaries were surprised in particular at the number of people who used the line. Company dividends were never less than 8 per cent, and this demonstration that a railway could be operated successfully led to a rush of similar schemes (source 149). In the following year, Stephenson's engines were used on the first public line in Scotland, linking the Monkland coalfield with Glasgow.

The railway age had begun.

ABOVE: Stephenson experienced great engineering problems in building the Liverpool-Manchester Railway. Here is his solution to the problem of crossing Chat Moss

ABOVE: The cutting at Olive Mount
on the Liverpool-Manchester line

## SOURCE 142 Support for a railway

It has frequently occurred to me of late, that an iron rail-way, from London to Edinburgh (passing near to all the commercial towns of Leicester, Nottingham, Sheffield, Wakefield, Leeds, &c. &c. with branch rail-ways to Birmingham, Bristol, Manchester, and Liverpool, &c. &c.), would be productive of incalculable advantage to the country at large; and here I would suggest the propriety of making the first essay between Manchester and Liverpool, which would employ many thousands of the distressed population of that county.

The conveyance of the inland mails might be effected at a very trifling charge, compared with the present enormous expense of mailcoaches, as one coach upon a proper construction would take all the mails on the line of road between London and Edinburgh.

The introduction of fresh fish into the interior of the kingdom would open a source of trade to an immense number of individuals, and very essentially contribute to the improvements of our fisheries as well as to the establishment of new ones.

Very great benefit would arise to all estates in the direction of the rail-ways, by the very easy and cheap conveyance to market towns, but more especially to the metropolis, where provisions and vegetables of all kinds might be sent from distant parts of the kingdom.

T. Gray, *Observations on a General Iron Rail-way*, Baldwin, 1823, pp. xi-xii

## SOURCE 143 The opening of the Stockton-Darlington line

September 27 1825 The Stockton and Darlington railway was formally opened by the proprietors for the use of the public . . . The novelty of the scene, and the fineness of the day, had attracted an immense concourse of spectators, the fields on each side of the railway being literally covered with ladies and gentlemen on horseback, and pedestrians of all kinds. The train of carriages was then attached to a locomotive engine, built by Mr George Stephenson, in the following order: 1. Locomotive engine, with the engineer (Mr George Stephenson) and assistants. 2. Tender, with coals and water; next, six waggons, laden with coals and flour; then an elegant covered coach, with the committee and other proprietors of the railway; then 21 waggons, fitted up for passengers; and last of all, six waggons laden with coal, making altogether, a train of 38 carriages . . . Tickets were distributed to the number of near 300, but such was the pressure and crowd, that both loaded and empty carriages were instantly filled with passengers. The signal being given; the engine started off . . . and such was its velocity that, in some parts, the speed was frequently 12 miles [19 km] an hour, and in one place 15 miles [24 km] an hour . . . The engine, with its load, arrived in Darlington, a distance of 8¾ miles [14 km] in 65 minutes . . . By the time the cavalcade arrived at Stockton, where it was received with great joy, there were not less than 600 persons within, and hanging by the carriages. Part of the workmen were entertained at Stockton and part at Yarm; and there was a grand dinner for the proprietors and their most distinguished guests, to the number of 102, at the Town-hall in Stockton.

John Sykes, *Local Records . . . of Northumberland and Durham*, 1866, pp. 187-8

## SOURCE 144 Results of railways in the Darlington area

In addition to the social advantages which accrued from increased communication—and who shall doubt the fireside union, the social pleasure, and the domestic happiness it conferred?—was the development of commerce, and the increased importance of the various places through which it passed. A new trade in lime arose; the carriage in lead was enormously reduced in cost; the price of coal fell from 18s. to 8s. 6d.; the landholders received large sums for gravel, timber, and stone, taken from their estates. An obscure fishing village was changed into a considerable seaport town. The Stockton and Darlington railway turned the shop-keeper into a merchant, erected an exchange; gave bread to hundreds; and conferred happiness on thousands.

J. Francis, *A History of the English Railway*, Longman, 1851, Vol. I, pp. 56-7

## SOURCE 145 The need for a railway between Liverpool and Manchester

The distance between Liverpool and Manchester, by the Mersey and Irwell, exceeds 50 miles [80 km]; which cannot be performed in one day, and, as we have seen, requires some times many days. By a rail-road the distance is reduced to 33 miles [52.8 km], which would always be performed, whether by horses or engines, within the day; by the latter, the same engine would go and return with ease the same day, and be subject

ABOVE: The viaduct which had to be built over the River Irwell; another construction problem on the Liverpool-Manchester line

neither to delay nor risk of damage, nor total loss by adverse winds and storms which, on the passage of 18 miles [29 km] in the tide-way of the Mersey, frequently occur, nor would frost or drought interrupt the conveyance. Instead of 15s. per ton, the conveyance on the rail-road will only cost 10s. and probably less. By the establishment of a rail-way, the inhabitants of Liverpool will be entitled to buy their coals several shillings per ton below the price which they now pay. By opening the collieries to the sea, Liverpool will become one of the greatest shipping ports for coal in the kingdom. A rail-road will facilitate the conveyance of this indispensible article, together with the agricultural produce, the iron, limestone etc., throughout the whole manufacturing districts of Lancashire . . . Nor are the advantages of a rail-way merely of a local nature. By means of it and steam boats, the passage from Manchester to Dublin will be reduced to eighteen or twenty hours; . . . and by this rail-road, the rate at which the corn, the flax, the linen, and the butter of Ireland can be distributed in Lancashire and Yorkshire, will be considerably reduced. Among the plans for bettering the condition of Ireland, the Liverpool rail-road must be considered to take a prominent station, and the people of Ireland feel that it will do so.

*Quarterly Review*, 1825, Vol. 31, pp. 375-6

## SOURCE 146  The problems of surveying

I was threatened to be ducked in the pond if I proceeded, and, of course, we had a great deal of the survey to take by stealth, at the time when the people were at dinner. We could not get it done by night; indeed we were watched day and night, and guns were discharged over the grounds belonging to Captain Bradshaw to prevent us.

S. Smiles, *Story of the Life of George Stephenson*, Murray, 1862, p. 156

## SOURCE 147  Opposition to the Liverpool and Manchester Railway

When the bill went into committee, the opposition was strong and severe. Satire and argument were alike brought to bear upon the subject. The witnesses were subjected to a severe cross examination; Mr Stephenson was attacked with an undeserved severity; the claims of the land-owner were placed in a prominent position; the locomotive was laughed at, the speed was denied, and the Exchange of Liverpool denounced for having aided and abetted so preposterous a plan . . .

Vegetation, it was prophesied, would cease wherever the locomotive passed. The value of land would be lowered by it; the market gardener would be ruined by it; the market could carry goods cheaper. Steam would vanish before storm and frost; property would be deteriorated near a station . . . It was erroneous, impracticable, and unjust. It was a great and scandalous attack on private property, upon public grounds.

J. Francis, *A History of the English Railway*, Longman, 1851, Vol. I, pp. 106-7

BELOW: Travelling on the Liverpool–
Manchester Railway

| | From 16th Sept to 31st Dec. 1830. | From 1st Jan. to 30th June, 1831. | From 1st July to 31st Dec. 1831. | From 1st Jan. to 30th June, 1832. | From 1st July to 31st Dec. 1832. | From 1st Jan. to 30th June, 1833. |
|---|---|---|---|---|---|---|
| | Tons. | Tons. | Tons. | Tons. | Tons. | Tons. |
| Merchandise between Liverpool and Manchester . | 1,433 | 35,865 | 52,224 | 54,174 | 61,995 | 68,284 |
| Road Traffic . . | .. | 373 | 2,347 | 3,707 | 6,011 | 8,712 |
| Between Liverpool and Bolton Junction . . . . | .. | 6,827 | 10,917 | 14,720 | 18,836 | 19,461 |
| Coal . . . . | 2,630 | 2,889 | 8,396 | 29,456 | 39,940 | 41,375 |
| Passengers booked at Company's offices . | No. 71,951 | No. 188,726 | No. 256,321 | No. 174,122 | No. 182,823 | No. 171,421 |
| Number of Trips— | | | | | | |
| With Passengers . | No Acc. | 2,259 | 2,944 | 2,636 | 3,363 | 3,262 |
| With Goods . . | .. | 1,873 | 2,298 | 2,248 | 1,679 | 2,244 |
| With Coal . . . | .. | 293 | 150 | 234 | 211 | 164 |

| | From 1st July to 31st Dec. 1833. | From 1st Jan. to 30th June, 1834. | From 1st July to 31st Dec. 1834. | From 1st Jan. to 30th June, 1835. | From 1st July to 31st Dec. 1835. | From 1st Jan. to 30th June, 1836. |
|---|---|---|---|---|---|---|
| | Tons. | Tons. | Tons. | Tons. | Tons. | Tons. |
| Merchandise between Liverpool and Manchester . | 69,806 | 69,522 | 72,577 | 76,448 | 79,114 | 81,415 |
| Road Traffic . . | 9,733 | 15,201 | 11,482 | 12,282 | 15,015 | 14,983 |
| Between Liverpool and Bolton Junction . . . . | 18,708 | 19,633 | 22,321 | 24,917 | 22,853 | 21,219 |
| Coal . . . . | 40,134 | 46,039 | 53,298 | 55,444 | 60,802 | 68,893 |
| Passengers booked at Company's offices . | No. 215,071 | No. 200,676 | No. 235,961 | No. 205,741 | No. 268,106 | No. 202,848 |
| Number of Trips— | | | | | | |
| With Passengers . | 3,253 | 3,317 | 3,325 | 3,222 | 3,347 | 3,353 |
| With Goods . . | 2,587 | 2,499 | 2,108 | 2,091 | 2,132 | 2,157 |
| With Coal . . . | 37 | 32 | 161 | 355 | 473 | 536 |

ABOVE: Contemporary statistics show the success of the Liverpool-Manchester line

## SOURCE 148 Chat Moss

No engineer in his senses would go through Chat Moss if he wanted to make a railroad from Liverpool to Manchester . . . The surface of the Moss is a sort of long, coarse sedgy grass, tough enough to enable you to walk upon it, about half-leg deep. In the centre, where this railroad is to cross, it is all pulp from the top to the depth of 34 feet [10 m]; at 34 feet there is a vein of 4 or 6 inches [10–15 cm] of clay; below that there are 2 or 3 feet (60–80 cm] of quicksand; and the bottom of that is hard clay, which keeps all the water in.

Evidence of Francis Giles to the Parliamentary Committee on the Liverpool and Manchester Railway Bill, in Smiles, *The Life of George Stephenson*, pp. 169–70

## SOURCE 149 The success of the Liverpool-Manchester line

The great success attending this splendid work being in a principal degree attributable to the passengers conveyed by it, the chief inducement thenceforward to embark in similar undertakings has been the number of travellers and not the amount of goods to be conveyed. Hitherto it has been found, in nearly every case where a railroad adapted for carrying passengers has been brought into operation, that the amount of travelling between the two extremities of the line has been quadrupled. In the case of the Liverpool and Manchester Railway, the income derived from this source has enabled the Company to meet a large amount of extraordinary expenses, and to divide regularly 10 per cent annually upon the capital, although the outlay in the construction of the work has been more than double the sum contemplated in the original estimates.

G. R. Porter, *The Progress of the Nation*, H. Bohn, 1838, p. 65

# Growth of the system

Following the success of the Liverpool-Manchester line, numerous companies were formed and by 1851, a national network of sorts had been developed (source 150 and Map p.151).

We shall see later that this network developed in spite of engineering and financial problems. However, before work could even start on a line, there was nearly always some local opposition to overcome Sometimes opposition was trivial, but it all had to be taken seriously by the railway companies, and a public debate often accompanied the early stages of a railway project (sources 151-153).

One railway scheme which met stronger opposition than many was Isambard Kingdom Brunel's Great Western Railway. Landowners like Countess Berkeley claimed that their homes would become uninhabitable if the line were constructed; farmers feared Irish competition once produce could be transported easily from Bristol; the Kennet and Avon Canal denounced the scheme; and even Eton College and Oxford University resisted a project which they felt would bring danger to students at Eton, and in Oxford's case, destroy the peace of a city devoted to learning (source 154).

Yet, despite this opposition and at a cost of £6·5 millions, the Great Western Railway was built, and with the completion of the famous Box Tunnel in 1841, London was linked to Bristol.

Unlike the lines that had been built in other parts of the country, Brunel used a seven foot (2·134 m) Broad Gauge for his railway, claiming that the wider wheel base would allow greater safety at high speeds as well as more roomy carriages. Inevitably this resulted in problems where Standard (1·231 m) and Broad Gauge lines met, since both passengers and goods had to change trains.

## Amalgamation

Apart from granting permission to build a line, Parliament took little part in the building of the early railways. Therefore lines were built without much thought for coordinating services, equipment or even track. A Railway Department of the Board of Trade was set up in 1840 which inspected newly constructed lines before they were opened. And, as we shall see, the Railway Act of 1844 improved railway services. Otherwise, improvements in the railway network were left to the companies themselves. One method of achieving this in the 1840s was through the amalgamation of separate lines.

1844 to 1847 saw a mania for building new lines (source 155)

It became clear to some companies that there would be both profit and benefit in trying to create a system out of the patchwork of local lines. In 1844, the Midland Railway, linking Rugby with South Yorkshire, had been formed by the amalgamation of three separate lines. In Scotland, the North British and the Caledonian railways were formed in the same way. Other schemes followed.

To contemporaries, the outstanding figure in this 'railway mania' was George Hudson, 'the Railway King'. Starting as a York linen draper, Hudson became involved in railways and through building, buying and amalgamation, built up his own empire—the North Eastern Railway. By 1846, he controlled 1000 miles (1600 km) of railway. However, Hudson's financial methods were eventually questioned and when it was discovered that he had been paying dividends out of capital, he was disgraced. Nevertheless, Hudson's achievement pointed the way to a national system.

ABOVE: Isambard Kingdom Brunel

ABOVE: George Hudson,
'Railway King'

## SOURCE 150 Railway mileage 1825-51

| Year | Miles opened each year | | | | | | |
|---|---|---|---|---|---|---|---|
| 1825 | 27 | 1834 | 90 | 1843 | 105 |
| 1826 | 11 | 1835 | 40 | 1844 | 192 |
| 1827 | 3 | 1836 | 66 | 1845 | 288 |
| 1828 | 4 | 1837 | 137 | 1846 | 634 |
| 1829 | 6 | 1838 | 202 | 1847 | 712 |
| 1830 | 47 | 1839 | 227 | 1848 | 1253 |
| 1831 | 43 | 1840 | 528 | 1849 | 812 |
| 1832 | 26 | 1841 | 277 | 1850 | 621 |
| 1833 | 42 | 1842 | 164 | 1851 | 256 |

H. Pollins, *Britain's Railways*, David & Charles, 1971, pp. 28, 40

## SOURCE 151 Canal opposition

That they will meet with opposition from the two parties most interested in preserving their monopoly it is but natural to expect; . . . all persons interested in canals may probably unite their forces . . . concluding that, if they succeed in quashing this, they will be secure against all the others. We cannot anticipate the ground which may be taken in opposition . . . but it may rely upon the assumed ignorance, the private prejudices, interests, and relations of those who are to decide the question . . . The object may be to raise a clamour about 'vested rights', the invasion of private property, the crossing of turnpike roads, rivers, brooks and canals; passing through parks, avenues woods and grounds, occupied by noblemen and gentlemen within a few hundred yards of their residence, annoying them with clouds of smoke from high-pressure engines, frightening the cattle from their pastures and the plough, and other nonsense of similar kind.

*Quarterly Review*, 1825, Vol. 31, p. 376

### SOURCE 152 Opposition at Scarborough

The inhabitants of the place are well pleased to see respectable people amongst them; but they have no wish for a greater influx of vagrants, and those who have no money to spend; and I am sure that our respectable visitors have no relish for either a railroad or the pleasure of such company; on the contrary, they generally express their disapprobation of the measure; and I have heard many of them say that if there is a railroad to Scarborough, they should never come again, as visitors on pleasure . . .

George Knowles, 'Observations on the Expediency of Making a Line of Railroad from York to Scarborough,' 1841, in E. W. Martin, *Country Life in England*, Macdonald, 1966, p. 167

### SOURCE 153 Opposition to Sunday working

During 1835 the scheme [a railway between Hull and Selby] gathered strength, and at a meeting in October, 1835 . . . it was announced that £135 000 had been subscribed. A great discussion, however, arose, led by the late Mr Avison Terry and the late Rev. John King as to whether the line, when made, was to be worked on Sundays or not, the argument used being—would the Merchants and Tradesmen who had subscribed open their counting houses and shops on Sunday? Many subscribers threatened to withdraw their subscriptions if the line was to be open on Sunday.

G. G. MacTurk, *A History of the Hull Railways*, Hull, 1879, p. 46

### SOURCE 154 Opposition to the Great Western Railway, 1834

The usual objection that it was the speculation of engineers, attorneys, and capitalists, was urged with the usual shallowness. The facilities of the railway could not be compared with those of the river. The people would be smothered in tunnels, and those that escaped suffocation would be burned in the carriages. Slopes were magnified into precipices, engines were to be upset, necks were to be broken. Eton College opposed it because it would be injurious to the discipline of the school, and dangerous to the morals of the pupils; and it was added, 'anybody who knew the nature of Eton boys, would know that they could not be kept from the railway.' A farmer objected to it because his cows might be killed in passing under an archway. A gentleman objected because no public benefit could compensate for destroying the beauties of his estate. The water

BELOW: Thomas Brassey (1805-70). The son of a Cheshire landowner, he started his career on the Grand Junction Railway. During the 30 years that followed he was involved in 90 construction schemes all over the world. By 1850 he was in control of an industrial army of 75 000 men, and the capital tied up in his various contracts amounted to some £36 million

in the Thames, remarked one, would be decreased, and the supply to Windsor Castle be destroyed.

Francis, *A History of the English Railway*, Vol. I, p. 214

### SOURCE 155 The railway mania

Three distinct lines were proposed to Norwich. Surrey was entirely mapped and marked out. All the opposition lines to Brighton were at a premium. In one parish of a metropolitan borough, sixteen schemes were afloat, and upwards of one thousand two hundred houses scheduled to be taken down... Railroads were advertised to places where no coaches ran. The Marquis of Londonderry stated that in Durham three railroads had been attempted by one projector, all running in parallel lines. One was at par, another was bankrupt, and he believed the third would never pay. The wildest schemes were calmly entertained. One projector proposed sails to propel his engine, and induced a company to try them. Another offered to propel his locomotives with rockets, confidently promising one hundred miles [160 km] an hour. A third invented a wooden line, to be raised many feet from the ground to allow a free ... passage beneath. Railways to carry invalids to bed were advertised, and a safety railway out of reach of injury was proposed.

Francis, *A History of the English Railway*, Vol. I, pp. 292-4

## Building the railways

Building railways was expensive. This was partly due to the initial cost of obtaining Parliament's permission to build a line. Where there was opposition to a scheme, this process took longer, and costs were proportionately higher.

However, even before the matter reached Parliament money had to be spent in surveying the proposed line and preparing a case to persuade Parliament that a particular scheme was necessary (sources 156, 157).

Once permission had been granted, land had to be bought. Sometimes this proved to be impossible because of a landowner's opposition, and then expensive detours had to be made. This could create further problems where difficult and expensive engineering operations resulted.

The construction of the line was the responsibility of contractors like Thomas Brassey and Samuel Morton Peto. But the actual work of blasting tunnels, laying lines, and moving earth was done by navvies—tough workers from areas like

Lincolnshire, Ireland and the West Country. Working in small groups, these men lived with the railway (sources 158-160). Wherever they went, they earned the reputation of hard workers and hard livers. Some contractors looked after their navvies, but others exploited them, paying them monthly and keeping them short of money so that they found it hard to leave (sources 161-163).

LEFT: Blasting a tunnel

BELOW: A newspaper advertisement announcing the opening of a new line

## SOURCE 156 The cost of Parliamentary permission

Statement of Parliamentary expenses incurred in obtaining Acts of Incorporation for the following under-takings:

| | £ | s | d |
|---|---|---|---|
| London and Birmingham railway | 72 868 | 18 | 10 |
| Great Western | 88 710 | 10 | 11 |
| London and Southampton | 29 040 | 16 | 6 |
| Midland Counties | 28 776 | 1 | 5 |
| Birmingham and Gloucester | 12 000 | 16 | 1 |
| Great North of England | 20 526 | 11 | 7 |
| Grand Junction | 22 757 | 10 | 4 |
| Bristol and Exeter | 18 592 | 1 | 10 |

Porter, *The Progress of the Nation*, p. 72

## HULL AND SELBY, OR HULL AND LEEDS JUNCTION, RAILWAY.

### OPENING OF THE LINE

#### FOR PASSENGERS AND PARCELS ONLY,

##### ON THURSDAY, JULY THE 2nd, 1840.

THE Public are respectfully informed that this RAILWAY IS OPENED THROUGH-OUT from HULL to the JUNCTION with the LEEDS and SELBY RAILWAY, at Selby, for the Carriage of PASSENGERS and PARCELS, presenting a direct Railway Conveyance from Hull to Selby, Leeds, and York, without change of Carriage.

TRAINS WITH PASSENGERS WILL START FROM HULL AS UNDER :

| AT SEVEN O'CLOCK, A.M. | AT THREE O'CLOCK, P.M. |
| AT TEN O'CLOCK, A.M. | AT SIX O'CLOCK, P.M. |

ON SUNDAYS, AT SEVEN O'CLOCK, A.M., AND SIX O'CLOCK, P.M.

The Trains from LEEDS and YORK will depart from those Places at the same Hours, *with the exception of the Evening Trains*, which will leave Leeds and York at SEVEN O'CLOCK, in order that the Passengers leaving London at Nine o'clock in the Morning may arrive in Hull at Half-past Nine o'Clock the same Evening. The Trains will leave YORK and LEEDS on SUNDAY EVENINGS at SIX O'CLOCK.

Passengers and Parcels may be Booked through at the Leeds, York, and Hull Stations. Arrangements have been made for forwarding Passengers to Sheffield, Derby, Birmingham, London, &c., by the Trains which leave Hull at Seven and Ten A.M.

There are no Trains from Hull at 11 A.M. and 5 15 P.M. as Advertised by the North Midland and Midland Counties Railway Companies, and owing to an alteration just made by those Companies, Passengers cannot at present be forwarded from Hull to London by the Train at 3 P.M.

THE FARES TO BE CHARGED ARE AS UNDER :

| | First Class. | Second Class. | Third Class. |
| Hull to Selby | 4s. 6d. | 4s. 0d. | 2s. 6d. |
| Hull to York | 8s. 0d. | 6s. 6d. | 4s. 6d. |
| Hull to Leeds | 8s. 0d. | 6s. 6d. | 4s. 6d. |

No Fees are allowed to be taken by the Guards, Porters, or any other Servants of the Company.

The Trains, both up and down will call at the Stations on the Line, viz. :—Hessle, Ferriby, Brough, Staddlethorpe, Eastrington, Howden, and Cliff.

Arrangements for conveying Goods, Cattle, Sheep, &c., will be completed in a short time, of which due Notice will be given.

By Order,

GEORGE LOCKING, Secretary.

*Railway Office, Hull, July 3rd, 1840.*

## SOURCE 157 Convincing Parliament

'Traffic-taking' was a curious employment. I remember when a schoolboy going into an inn in a remote part of North Yorkshire with two or three others. A seedy individual sat in the window, and immediately entered a note of our passing in a large book. He was one of the large army of traffic-takers sent out by some scheme, and his business was to sit for weeks in the inn window and score down all cattle, coaches and carriages, and people on foot passing the live long day, and perhaps a few imaginary ones if the case were urgent, and it was desirable to report to the Parliamentary Committee that an 'immense traffic' was waiting for the Universal Railway.

MacTurk, *A History of the Hull Railway*, p. 90

## SOURCE 158 How Brassey worked

When Mr Brassey took any contract, he let out portions of the work to sub-contractors. His way of dealing with them was this: he generally furnished all the materials, and all the plant. I find him on one occasion ordering as many as 2400 waggons from Messrs. Ransome and May. He also provided the horses. The sub-contractors contracted for the manual labour alone . . . I find that the sub-contracts varied from £5000 to £25 000 and that the number of men employed upon them would be from one to three hundred.

A. Helps, *The Life and Labours of Mr Brassey*, London, 1872, p. 47

## SOURCE 159 How the navvies worked

Joining together in a 'butty gang', some ten or twelve of these men would take a contract to cut out and remove so much 'dirt' . . . fixing their price according to the character of the 'stuff', and the distance to which it had to be wheeled and tipped. The contract taken, every man put himself to his mettle. If any was found skulking, or not putting forth his full-working power, he was ejected from the gang.

Smiles, *Life of George Stephenson*, p. 248

LEFT: A railway navvy

## SOURCE 160 How the navvies lived

They were in a state of utter barbarism. They made their homes where they got their work. Some slept in huts constructed of damp turf, cut from the wet grass, too low to stand upright in; while small sticks, covered with straw, served as rafters. Barns were better places than the best railway labourers' dwellings. Others formed a room of stones without mortar, placed thatch or flags across the roof, and took possession of it with their families, often making it a source of profit by lodging as many of their fellow-workmen as they could crowd into it. It mattered not to them that the rain beat through the roof, and that the wind swept through the holes. If they caught a fever, they died; if they took an infectious complaint, they wandered in the open air, spreading the disease wherever they went. In these huts they lived; with the space overcrowded; with man, woman and child mixing in promiscuous guilt; with no possible separation of the sexes; in summer wasted by unwholesome heats, and in winter literally hewing their way to their work through the snow. In such places from nine to fifteen hundred men were crowded for six years. Living like brutes, they were depraved, degraded, and reckless. Drunkenness and dissoluteness of morals prevailed. There were many women, but few wives.

Francis, *A History of the English Railway*, Vol. II, pp. 70-72

### SOURCE 161 'Tommy Shops' for the navvies

The . . . contractor raised a little city of turf huts, and accommodated his workmen on the spot. Their daily wants were met by the ticket system, or what was better known as the 'Tommy-shop'. Near the labourers' shanties was provided an emporium, furnished with all that their habits led them to procure. Ale in abundance, spirits, bread, meat, fat bacon, tobacco, shovels, jackets, gay crimson and purple waistcoats, boots, hats and night-caps, were all to be obtained at the convenient 'tommy-shop' keeper, who was a mere nominee and dependent of the contractor . . . Credit was always at their command. Even the newly-arrived and penniless 'navvy', provided that his boots were sound, could obtain a shovel on credit . . . Sometimes tickets say for five shillings each, would be issued to the workmen on account of wages, and the expenditure at the shop would be arranged, so as to exhaust these tickets by two or three settlements in a week.

The pay was generally monthly. On a large sheet, the detail and the total of every man's time, calculated in quarter days, was entered by the contractor's time-keeper or chief accountant. The rate of wages, varying for earth workmen from 2s. 6d. to 4s. 9d. per day, was added. The total earnings of the month thus arrived at were entered in the next column. In the following one came the amount drawn on tickets, or shop credit. The final column contained the cash balance due to the workman. It was extraordinary to see with how small an amount of actual specie the monthly pay was discharged. How much of that specie was to be melted into liquor within the next three days, was matter of very safe estimate. In fact, an argument by which the contractors met the desire of the Engineer that the workmen should be paid weekly, or at the farthest fortnightly, was that as they never resumed work till they had drunk out the balance of their earnings, it saved time and expedited the progress of the works to render these seasons of interruption as few as possible.

A Civil Engineer, *Personal Recollection of English Engineers*, 1868, pp. 181-3

## SOURCE 162  A strike

The navvies employed on the line of the Hull and Bridlington railway in the neighbourhood of Driffield on Monday morning last struck for an advance of wages. Great dissatisfaction also prevails on account of the contractors of the line paying the men in tickets on certain tradesmen for victuals instead of money as well as on account of settling with the men once a month.

*Hull Advertiser*, 17 September 1842

## SOURCE 163  Better conditions for navvies

1287. *What provision do you make as to lodgings for the men?*
In districts where we cannot get lodgings, we build what we call barracks for them.
1288. *What is the nature of the buildings; these barracks?*
We put up temporary wooden buildings, with a room for cooking, etc., and a long sleeping room on each side for the men; and then my plan is this: the agent selects a man who is steady and well conducted, and who has a wife, and allocates to him perhaps 25 men; and then he is provided with hammocks from our stores, which he is

bound to return in good condition at the end of the job, the same as they have on board ship; they congregate in the centre of their cooking-room, and on each side there are these hammocks slung; and these men have the use of the hammocks, and are charged a shilling a week.

1289. *The wife cooks for the whole of them?*

Yes.

1290. *You do not allow any other women in the barracks?*

No. The Honourable Members will see that 25s. a week for the trouble of cooking and making the beds would be an ample consideration for all their trouble, and an encouragement to good conduct in others. I get nothing at all; I put up the building and take it away.

1291. *But as to the wear and tear?*

That is my affair, and is calculated when I take the contract.

1292. *What is the largest number of men you ever accommodated?*

I had a large contract where 4000 men were employed, and I had to lodge a third of them.

Evidence of Samuel Morton Peto to the Select Committee on Railway Labourers, 1846; in
M. W. Flinn, *Readings in Economic and Social History*, Macmillan, 1965, pp. 275-6

RIGHT: Railway construction at Blackfriars, London

## Travel by rail

The railways were a novelty, and when a new line opened people rushed to use the new service (source 164).

The speed and cheapness of railway travel was what really impressed people, and the newspapers of the time frequently contained stories of people making what seemed very long journeys in next to no time. In fact, although one of the results of railways was to force canals to lower their freight charges, it was still cheaper for people to travel by water—assuming that time was no object (sources 165, 166).

THE RAILWAY—FIRST CLASS.

SECOND CLASS.

Most lines had three classes of railway carriage, though not all lines provided third class accommodation before 1844. First class carriages usually had roofs, windows and seats, but they were small and cramped. One of the main complaints about second class carriages seems to have been that they were draughty. The worst carriages, naturally, were the third class. For about 1p per kilometre, the public was allowed to travel in open trucks, the only protection from the weather being sides of about one metre in height. There were no seats, and carriage buffers were made of solid wood. Not surprisingly, people were increasingly critical of third class travel (source 167).

Eventually, Parliament intervened. In 1844, the Railways Act was passed. Amongst other things, it said that Railway Companies had to improve third class facilities (source 168).

THIRD CLASS.

ABOVE: The three classes of travel on the Liverpool-Manchester line

RAILWAY UNDERTAKING.

*Touter.* "Going by this Train, Sir?"      *Passenger.* "M? Eh? Yes."
*Touter.* "Allow me, then, to give you one of my Cards, Sir."

ABOVE: The break of gauge at
Gloucester. The broad gauge line of
the Great Western Railway met the
standard gauge of the Birmingham
line at Gloucester

ABOVE RIGHT: A *Punch* cartoon gives a
pessimistic view of railway travel

Apart from the discomfort of much
railway travel, the existence of many
separate companies meant that long-
distance travellers often had to change
trains; and one company's timetable might
pay no heed to that of another company.
For example, before 1844, a third class
traveller from London to Liverpool would
have discovered that there was only one
third class train in 24 hours. In addition, he
would have faced a long wait in
Birmingham for a second train to take him
on to Liverpool.

Further delays could be expected since
railway engines were still quite new and
breakdowns were frequent (source 169).
Accidents were also fairly common in
the early days, though the majority were
not serious. Some people who thought
of trains as rather like stagecoaches were
killed when they fell from riding on top of
a carriage; others were injured when they
jumped from a moving train in pursuit of a
hat. Another common cause of death was
the result of people being run over as they
lay drunk or asleep on the line. But the most
usual type of accident was a collision.

Yet despite possible inconvenience, discomfort, danger and delay, railway travel was both successful and popular. The numbers of people using the railways increased year after year (source 170).

## SOURCE 164 Early popularity

In the afternoon of Tuesday, the carriages made their first afternoon trip to Selby. The applicants for places were more numerous than the carriages were capable of accommodating, and a great number were disappointed of their anticipated pleasure. At about half past two the train left the yard of the Rail-Road and moved in fine order, at the rate of twenty miles [32 km] per hour. The speed subsided for a short time to about fifteen miles [24 km] per hour, and again increased to its former pace. In the first four days, seven hundred and seventy-nine persons travelled to Selby from Leeds, and seven hundred and forty-one to Leeds from Selby. The receipts from passengers in the course of those days amounted to one hundred and seventy-eight pounds.

E. Parsons, *Tourist Companion from Leeds and Selby to Hull*, Whittaker, 1835

## SOURCE 165 The speed of railways

Travelling upon this road [the Leeds–Selby railway] continues to increase. It is not at all an unusual thing to leave Hull at 7 o'clock in the morning with the steam packets and to arrive in Leeds by railway at 12 o'clock the same day. On Tuesdays and Saturdays when the last train on the Manchester and Liverpool railway leaves the station at Manchester at 6 o'clock in the evening a person leaving Hull at 7 o'clock in the morning and availing himself of the rapidity of the 2 railways arrives at Liverpool at half past 7 in the evening having travelled in 12 hours and a half 155 miles [248 km].

*Hull Advertiser*, 9 February 1841

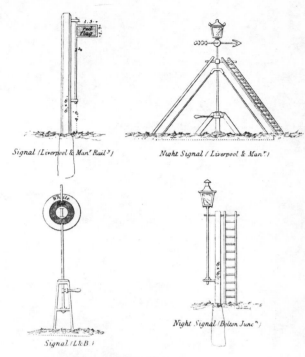

Signal (Liverpool & Man' Rail')

Night Signal (Liverpool & Man')

Signal (L&B)

Night Signal (Bolton Junc")

ABOVE: The early signalling system was inefficient. Signals were operated by hand, and were sometimes difficult to see

## SOURCE 166 Comparative costs, 1844

**By Canal boat,** Manchester to London

| | £ | s | d |
|---|---|---|---|
| 2 adults' passage, 14s. each | 1 | 8 | 0 |
| 8 children's passage, 7s. each | 1 | 1 | 0 |
| Provisions, etc. for 5 days' passage, 5s. each | 1 | 5 | 0 |
| **Total** | **3** | **14** | **0** |

**By Coach,** Manchester to London, 186 miles [297.6 km]

| | £ | s | d |
|---|---|---|---|
| 2 adults' passage, 30s. each | 3 | 0 | 0 |
| 8 children's passage, 15s. each | 2 | 5 | 0 |
| Coachmen and Guard | | 7 | 0 |
| Food etc. | | 10 | 0 |
| **Total** | **6** | **2** | **0** |

**By Railway,** Manchester to London, 212 miles [339.2 km]

| | £ | s | d |
|---|---|---|---|
| Third-class, Manchester to Birmingham, | | | |
| 2 adults' passage, 11s. each | 1 | 2 | 0 |
| 3 children's passage, 5s. 6d. each | | 16 | 6 |
| Third-class, Birmingham to London, | | | |
| 2 adults' passage, 14s. each | 1 | 8 | 0 |
| 3 children's passage, 7s. each | 1 | 1 | 0 |
| Food etc., 1s. 6d. each | | 7 | 6 |
| **Total** | **4** | **15** | **0** |

Appendix No. 4, *Report of Select Committee on Railways*, 1844; in W. T. Jackman, *The Development of Transportation in Modern England*, Cambridge University Press, 1916, p. 606

BELOW: Inside a third class suburban railway carriage

## SOURCE 167 Third class travel

Earl Dalhousie said in the House of Peers . . . that the third-class traffic had been a disgrace to railway companies, and if continued, would be a still greater discredit to the parliament which allowed it. The committee had recommended the House of Commons to require from all railway companies that there should be upon every line at convenient times, and with proper accommodation, carriages, with seats defended from the weather, for third-class passengers.

Some of the companies compelled third-class passengers to travel whole days without seats, making them, in a journey which might not occupy more than seven hours and a-half, stand on their feet sixteen or seventeen hours.

Francis, *A History of the English Railway*, Vol. II, p. 98

## SOURCE 168 'Parliamentary Trains'

11. That the Companies may be required to provide upon such new Lines of Railway, as a minimum of third-class accommodation, one Train at least each way on every week-day, by which there shall be the ordinary obligation to convey such passengers as may present themselves at any of the ordinary stations, in carriages provided with seats and protected from the weather, at a speed not less than 12 miles an hour [19 km] including stoppages, and at fares not exceeding a penny per mile; each Passenger by such Train being allowed not exceeding 56 lbs. [26 kg] of luggage without extra charge, and extra luggage being charged by weight at a rate not exceeding the lowest charge by other Trains: Children under Three years being conveyed without extra charge; and Children from Three to Twelve years at half-price.

Resolution presented by the Select Committee on Railways, 1844, in G. M. Young & W. D. Handcock, *English Historical Documents 1833-74*, Eyre & Spottiswoode, 1956, p. 249

## SOURCE 169 Breakdowns on the North Midland line

**Jan. 2nd.**—No. 48 engine, sent out to bring in a broken horse-box; connecting rod broke, and that broke the cylinder cover and otherwise seriously damaged the working gear.

**Jan. 3rd.**—Before the goods train out of Leeds at 8 p.m. arrived at Masbro'—a distance of thirty-two miles [51 km]—the driver was compelled to draw his fire out. He afterwards arrived at Derby six hours late. (This engine-man only worked a stationary engine before.) The eight o'clock into Derby overtook a coal train about three miles [4.8 km] from Derby with four engines attached to it, the gatekeeper informing the alarmed and trembling passengers that it was only a coal train that had obstructed the line for five hours. The cause of employing so many engines was that three of them were sent out as pilots, one after the other, but unfortunately got so disabled themselves that they were unable to render the necessary assistance.

**Jan. 4th.**—No. 61 engine, running the coke train, broke down in Killamarsh Cutting. No. 44 engine, having undergone a thorough repair, broke one of the cylinders, and was otherwise much damaged. No. 6 engine, running the mail train, broke the connecting rod.

**Jan. 5th.**—No. 11 engine, running the mail train out of Derby, broke down after running eight miles [12 km]; with all the energy possible, it cannot be put into a proper state of repair for months. This caused a delay to the mail of two hours and twelve minutes into Leeds. No. 9 engine, damaged very much in the fire-box. The 10.15 train into Derby broke down, and was unable to proceed till the 11.15 train came and brought both trains into Derby; damage serious.

**Jan. 6th.**—The 3.15 train out of Derby broke down and was taken into Leeds by the pilot engine; one hour fifty minutes late.

*Railway Times*, January 1843

## SOURCE 170 Railway passengers 1838 and 1843-51

| Year | Millions of passengers carried |
|------|-------------------------------|
| 1838 | 5.4 |
| 1843 | 21.7 |
| 1844 | 25.2 |
| 1845 | 30.4 |
| 1846 | 40.2 |
| 1847 | 47.9 |
| 1848 | 54.4 |
| 1849 | 57.8 |
| 1850 | 67.4 |
| 1851 | 79.7 |

B. R. Mitchell & P. Deane, *Abstract of British Historical Statistics*, Cambridge University Press, 1971, p. 225

# The impact of railways

It was not difficult to predict that railways would bring great changes to peoples' lives. A lot of these changes were beneficial, but some people had cause to dislike the railways. Many of the landowners who had at first opposed the railways soon found that it was good to have swift and cheap transport nearby. But people connected with other forms of transport found that competition made life hard. Canal companies were forced to cut their freight charges, but even then they could not compete. On the roads, coach companies, inns and turnpike trusts suffered (sources 171-173).

BELOW: A number of towns developed rapidly as a direct result of the railways. Some were important junctions, while others developed round new railway works. This picture shows Swindon in the early days of the Great Western Railway

ABOVE: The Grand Junction Railway Fete, held to mark the emergence of the 'juvenile city' of Crewe

Crewe developed rapidly and other towns like Derby and Newcastle grew as the railways demanded more and more resources and equipment (sources 174, 175).

Increasingly, these demands were magnified by the construction of lines by British engineering companies in other countries (source 176).

Employment was provided indirectly for steelworkers, miners, forestry workers and many others. But work was also created for the men and women who actually ran the railways—from the train driver to the man who creosoted railway sleepers (source 177).

Some contemporaries believed that the railways had most impact on the workers and the poor. And it is easy to see that town dwellers would benefit from new jobs, leisure excursions and the new experiences railways provided (sources 178-180).

But the influence of railways was much wider. Perhaps the most important long-term result was that railways put people 'in touch'—with events, with places, with one another.

Cheap fish for dinner would have been seen by a Black Country locksmith as an obvious result of railway transport. But the same man might also have been involved in Radical politics, and so the railways could well have affected his life in another way. Different parts of the country seemed to move together as the

Railways encouraged market gardening and helped improve people's diet: perishable foods such as fish could reach a market quickly, though not everyone agreed that this ease of transport was a benefit. Growing fishing ports like Grimsby and Aberdeen were not the only towns to change as a result of railways. New railway towns like Swindon and

## TRIPS FOR CHRISTMAS
### FOR 2, 3, 4, or 6 DAYS.
### ALL COVERED CARRIAGES!!

# A GRAND TRIP
### WILL LEAVE LEEDS, NORMANTON, AND CASTLEFORD,
## ON TUESDAY, DEC. 24th, 1850,
At Half-past 12 o'Clock at Noon, for

# HULL, YORK
# AND SCARBRO'.

| Stations the Train starts from. | Time. | TO YORK & BACK. Covered Carriages. | First Class. | TO HULL & BACK. Covered Carriages. | First Class. | TO SCARBRO' & BACK. Covered Carriages. | First Class. |
|---|---|---|---|---|---|---|---|
| LEEDS & WOODLESFORD,...... | Half-past...12 | 2 6 | 3 6 | 3 0 | 5 0 | 4 6 | 7 6 |
| NORMANTON & CASTLEFORD, | 40 min. past 12 | 2 0 | 3 0 | 2 6 | 4 6 | 4 0 | 6 0 |

### ORSERVE THE FOLLOWING PARTICULARS.

Tickets and Bills may be had at all the Railway Stations.
The Train from Leeds, will start from the Wellington Station, near the Commercial Buildings.
There will be no Open Carriage, but all Covered, for the Third Class Passengers. In order to do this, the Second Class Fare has been withdrawn for this Trip.
Passengers are requested to be at their respective Stations Fifteen Minutes before the time named on the Bills, as the Train will start from Leeds and Normanton as punctual as possible.
Passengers will go to Hull and York direct; but those for Scarbro', will stay in York about one hour and a half, to enable them to see the interesting places in that Ancient City; passengers can visit St. Mary's Abbey and Grounds, in which are the Two Beautiful Museums, by paying 3d. each, and showing their Trip Tickets.
Passengers for Scarbro', and Malton, will leave York by the Quick Train, which starts from York at Five Minutes to Four o'Clock; arriving in Scarbro' at a Quarter-past Five.

### NOTICE THE FOLLOWING PARTICULARS FOR RETURNING.

Trip Passengers can return from Hull, York, and Scarbro', on Wednesday the 25th, Thursday the 26th, Friday the 27th, Saturday the 28th, and Monday the 30th of December, by the Regular Train which leaves Hull at Two o'Clock in the Afternoon, Scarbro' at a Quarter-past Twelve in the Afternoon, and York at Ten Minutes past Three in the Afternoon.

### REMEMBER the Trip starts on Tuesday, the 24th of December, the Afternoon before Christmas Day, at Half-past Twelve o'Clock.

Tradesmen and others will much oblige by showing this Bill in their Window.

### T. CLAPHAM, 20, Commercial Buildings, Leeds.

C. A. WILSON & CO., LETTER-PRESS PRINTERS, SHERWOOD'S YARD 42, BRIGGATE, LEEDS.

---

travelling time between them decreased. Newspapers carried by rail brought people recent, national news, and the cheap mail service started in 1840 would scarcely have been possible without railways (sources 181, 182).

The development of a railway system, therefore, represented much more than a speeding-up of transport.

LEFT: Railways provided work in many less obvious ways. Here, seven men are creosoting sleepers
BELOW LEFT: An excursion poster. Scarborough was well established as a resort for the rich before the railways, but rail travel made it possible for all people who could afford the fare to visit the seaside

### SOURCE 171 A prediction for the future

Such a new power of locomotion cannot be introduced without working a vast change in the state of society. With so great a facility and celerity of communication, the provincial towns of an empire would become so many suburbs of the metropolis—or rather the effect would be similar to that of collecting the whole inhabitants into one city. Commodities, inventions, discoveries, opinions, would circulate with a rapidity hitherto unknown.

*The Scotsman*, 22 December 1825

### SOURCE 172 Canals and railways

On the introduction of railways . . . the consequent competition reduced the expense of conveyance. [There are] instances . . . in which the charges for conveyance of merchandise have been lowered by these means to one seventh of their former amount, and there are now few parts of the country which have not derived . . . advantage from the competition between railroads and canals . . .

. . . However, where effective competition has for a time been maintained, it has been attended with such a large reduction of profits that it has become the interest of the rival companies to combine for their mutual advantage, and hence have arisen private arrangements, under which a higher scale of tolls and charges has been re-established.

Extract from the *Report of a Select Committee on the Amalgamation of Railways and Canals, 1846*; quoted in Young & Handcock, *English Historical Documents 1833-74*, pp. 258-9

## SOURCE 173 Turnpike roads and the railways

131 *What situation do you hold?*
I am proprietor of the Bull and Mouth Inn and coach establishment.

132 *Would you state to the Committee whether or not of late, say within the last two or three years, you have experienced any result from the formation of railroads?*
I have a reduction on the North road since the opening of the railroad of 15 coaches daily . . .

161 *Do you attribute your losses to the formation of railroads entirely?*
Yes, entirely; our business was in a very fair state until then.

162 *You stated you anticipated taking away most of the coaches, except for one or two timid persons, who do not like to go by the railroad?*
What we carry now are mostly people who are timid people and do not like to go by the railroad, except when we go with very low fares indeed which induces the lower orders of people. These people are so poor the coachmen and the guards say they get nothing besides the passage money; their places are not worth having.

163 *They go only for the sake of cheapness, with whom time is no object?*
Yes, they are generally a very low order of people who go by us to save 3s. or 4s.

164 *As to timid people, do you not think when the railroads are generally used, that timidity will entirely go away?*
Daily we find out many people who would not have gone for any consideration, go now.

165 *You carry a good many parcels from London to Birmingham?*
They diminish as we cannot compete with the railway to time.

166 *What, in your opinion, will be the result of the railroad in reference to the travelling by the turnpike roads between London and Birmingham?*
It will be completely annihilated as to animal power; unless something more than even the duties and tolls being all taken clear away is done, we shall not be able to get a living.

Extracts from the evidence of Edward Sherman to the Select Committee on Turnpike Trusts, *Parliamentary Papers*, 1839, Vol. IX, 8–10

## SOURCE 174 Cattle prices

At a meeting of the Statistical Society a paper was read on the agricultural prices of the parishes of Middlesex. The writer proceeded to say that the railway had greatly affected prices in the cattle market at Southall and had occasioned much discontent among the farmers, who complained that, in consequence of the facility that it afforded for the rapid transfer of stock from one county to another, they had been deprived of the advantage which they had formerly possessed from their proximity to London. Five hundred head of sheep and 100 head of cattle had upon more than one occasion been suddenly introduced into the market from the West of England and prices had been proportionately forced down.

W. M. Acworth, *The Railways of England*, Murray, 1899, p. 27

## SOURCE 175 The demand for raw materials

80 000 000 train miles were run annually on the railways, 5000 engines and 150 000 vehicles composed the working stock. The engines, in a straight line, would extend from London to Chatham; the vehicles from London to Aberdeen; and the companies employed 90 400 officers and servants; whilst the engines consumed annually 2 000 000 tons of coal, so that in every minute of time four tons of coal flashed into steam twenty tons of water, an amount sufficient for the supply of the domestic and other wants of the town of Liverpool. The coal consumed was equal to the whole amount exported to foreign countries, and to one half of the annual consumption of London . . .

The wear and tear was great; 20 000 tons of iron required to be replaced annually; and 26 000 000 sleepers annually perished: 300 000 trees were annually felled to make good the loss of sleepers; and 300 000 trees could be grown on little less than 5000 acres of forest-land.

R. D. Baxter in *The Journal of the Royal Statistical Society*, 1866

## SOURCE 176 British railways abroad

We have covered with railroads the fairest districts of the United Kingdom, and developed railways in our colonies of Canada and India. But we have done much more than this, we have introduced them into almost every civilised country. To this day, wherever an undertaking of more than ordinary difficulty presents itself, the aid is invoked of English engineers, English contractors, English navvies, and English shareholders; and a large portion of the rails with which the line is laid, and the engines and rolling stock with which it is worked are brought from England.

Speech by Robert Stephenson published in *The Engineer*, January 1856, p. 15

## SOURCE 177 Railway companies and employment

Ninety thousand men were employed directly, and upwards of 40 000 collaterally; 130 000 men, with their wives and families, represented a population of 500 000 souls; so that 1 in 50 of the entire population of the Kingdom might be said to be dependent upon the railways!

Speech by Robert Stephenson published in *The Engineer*, January 1856, p. 15

BELOW: One of the army of railway workers. The railways themselves became a source of employment

ABOVE: This cartoon of 1850
comments on the craze for railway
excursions

ABOVE TOP: A workmen's train. The railways made it possible to travel greater distances to work
ABOVE: Engineering works at Newcastle-upon-Tyne. Railways started in the North-East

## SOURCE 178 The Magna Carta of movement

Now, who have specially benefited by this vast invention? The rich, whose horse and carriages carried them in comfort over the known world?—the middle classes to whom stage coaches and mails were an accessible mode of conveyance?—or the poor, whom the cost of locomotion condemned often to an almost vegetable existence? Clearly the latter. The rail-road is the Magna Carta of their motive freedom. How few among the last generation ever stirred beyond their own village? How few among the present will die without visiting London? . . . The number who left Manchester by cheap trips in one week of holiday time last year exceeded 202 000; against 150 000 in 1849, and 116 000 in 1848.

*The Economist*, 1851

## SOURCE 179 An excursion from Leeds

A fortnight ago we recorded the astonishing fact that no fewer than 6600 persons were conveyed from Leeds to Hull and back again in 20 hours—the first train leaving Hull at 6 o'clock in the morning and the last train arriving back again in Leeds at two o'clock on the following morning—in a train consisting of 4 divisions and comprising of 29 carriages and 9 engines . . .

It is a gratifying circumstance to see the means of rational enjoyment so eminently conducive to health thus brought within the power of the great majority of the people . . . and we rejoice to believe that the general prosperity of the last twelve months at least, will supply them with the means of enjoying many such excursions.

*Leeds Mercury*, 5 October 1844

## SOURCE 180 Railways and education

Railways have accomplished what the far-famed SOCIETY FOR THE DIFFUSION OF USEFUL KNOWLEDGE, with its long train of noble and ignoble patrons and its penny magazines and penny encyclopaedias . . . could never have effected; they have taught the through-bred Londoner ALMOST to discriminate between a plough and a harrow, and to recognise a potato by its stem.

*Railway Times*, 1837

## SOURCE 181 The railways and public opinion

The opening of the Manchester and Liverpool Railway was one of the events of 1830, which was not without its influence, in future days, on the progress of public opinion. The anti-corn law agitation was wonderfully forwarded by quick railway travelling and the penny postage. Even in 1830 the railway promoted the cause of reform . . . It brought a little propriety borough, which nobody had ever seen before, into full view. I recollect when passing over it, for the first time, I said to a friend: 'Parliamentary reform must follow soon after the opening of this road. A million of persons will pass over it this year and see that hitherto unseen little village of Newton; and they must be convinced of the absurdity of its sending two members to parliament, whilst Manchester sends none.'

Prentice, *Historical Sketches and Personal Recollections*, p. 369

## SOURCE 182 Cheap postage in a Suffolk village

As a specimen of the letters which I had received describing the commercial and social advantages of cheap postage, I read the following from Professor Henslow:

Hitcham, Hadleigh, Suffolk
16 April, 1843

Dear Sir,

To the importance of the penny postage to those who cultivate science I can bear testimony, as I am continually receiving and transmitting a variety of specimens, living and dead, by post. Among them I have received three living carnivorous slugs, which arrived safe in a pill-box . . . That the penny postage is an important addition to the comforts of the poor labourer I can also testify. From my residence in a neighbourhood where scarcely any labourer can read, much less write, I am often employed by them as an amanuensis, and have frequently heard them express their satisfaction at the facility they enjoy of now corresponding with distant relatives . . .

I remain, dear Sir, yours very faithfully,
(signed) J. S. Henslow

Rowland Hill, *The State and Prospects of Penny Postage*, Charles Knight, 1844, p. 84

Du = Dundee
G = Glasgow
E = Edinburgh

St = Stockton
Se = Selby

L = Leeds
M = Manchester

De = Derby
B = Birmingham

C = Cardiff
Sw = Swindon

0    km    100

**The Railway Network in 1851**

ABOVE: Frost Fair

# 5
# Broadsides and Ballads

## PETERLOO.

See! see! where freedom's noblest champion
    stands,
Shout! shout! illustrious patriot band,
Here grateful millions their generous tribute
    bring,
And shouts for freedom make the welkin
    ring,
While fell corruption and her hellish crew
The blood-stained trophies gained at Peter-
    loo.

Soon shall fair freedom's sons their right
    regain,
Soon shall all Europe join the hallowed
    strain,
Of Liberty and Freedom, Equal Rights and
    Laws,
Heaven's choicest blessing crown this glo-
    rious cause,
While meanly tyrants, crawling minions too,
Tremble at their feats performed on Peter-
    loo.

Britons, be firm, assert your rights, be bold,
Perish like heroes, not like slaves be sold,;
Firm and unite, bid millions be free,
Will to your children glorious liberty,
While cowards—despots long may keep in
    view,
And silent contemplate the deeds on Peterloo.

## The songs

The song on the right was published in 1819. What do you think its purpose was, and why do you think the publisher thought he could make money out of it?

In its published form this song is called a broadside ballad and if you had lived in the period we are studying, broadsides would have been very familiar to you. They were on sale everywhere and one writer, the actor and playwright Thomas Holcroft, commented that, 'even the walls of cottages and little alehouses . . . had old English ballads, such as *Death and the Lady*, and *Margaret's Ghost*, with lamentable tragedies, or *King Charles's golden rules*, occasionally pasted on them.'

However, broadsides were not all like the example about Peterloo. They did a variety of jobs; you will see this in looking at the following pages.

Broadsides were important to people because they provided popular songs to sing, and also topical tales, news of crimes and executions, information about political and religious controversies, stories of personal tragedies and even appeals to the new class of town-based workers. The various broadsides that people could buy did the job that records, television, newspapers, radio and film do for us today—and all for ½d a time!

During the period we are studying, almost anything could be bought on the streets, and this is where broadsides were purchased. They could be obtained at fairs or markets like the one shown here, but more usually they were sold in the street by peddlars or special salesmen called 'patterers' (source 183). Perhaps you can work out why they were given that name? The man on p.156 is a 'long-song seller' (source 184).

RIGHT: These two broadsides tell us about the way towns were growing and about wages and prices. Broadsides were often regional. There is another song called 'I can't find Brummagem' which tells much the same story as 'Manchester's an Altered Town'

# MANCHESTER'S

## AN

# ALTERED TOWN.

Once on a time this good old town was nothing but a village,
Of husbandry, and farmers too, whose time was spent in tillage;
But things are altered very much, such building now allotted is,
It rivals far and soon will leave behind the great Metropolis.
O dear O, Manchester's an altered town, O dear O.

Once on a time were you inclin'd, your weary limbs to lave, sir,
In summer's scorching heat in the Irwell's cooling wave, sir;
You had only got to go to the Old Church for the shore, sir,
But since those days the fish have died, and now they are no more,
sir.

When things do change you ne'er do know what next is sure to
follow,
For mark the change in Broughton now, of late 'twas but a hollow
For they have found it so snug, and chang'd its etymology,
They've clapt in it a wild beast's show, now call'd the Gardens
of Zoology.

A market on Shudehill was, and it remains there still, sir,
The Salford old bridge is taken away, and clapt a new one in, sir,
There's Newton lane I now shall name, has had an alteration,
They've knock'd a great part of it down, to make a railway station.

There's the Bolton railway station in Salford, give attention,
Besides many more too numerous to mention;
Besides a new Police, to put the old ones down stairs, sir,
A mayor and corporation to govern this old town, sir.

There's the Manchester and Salford old bridge, that long has stood,
the weather,
Because it was so very old they drown'd it altogether;
And Brown street market too, it forms part of this sonnet,
Down it must come, they say, to build a borough gaol upon it.

Not long ago if you had taken a walk thro' Stevenson's square, sir,
You might have seen, if you look'd, a kind of chapel there, sir,
And yet this place, some people thought, had better to come down,
sir,
And in the parson's place they put a pantaloon and clown, sir.

In former times our cotton swells were not half so mighty found, sir,
But in these modern times they everywhere abound, sir,
With new police and watchmen, to break peace there's none dare
And at every step the ladies go, policemen will cry, move on there'

In former days this good old town was guarded from the prigs, sir,
By day constables, by night by watchmen with Welsh wigs, sir;
But things are alter'd very much, for all those who are scholars,
May tell the new policemen by their numbers on their collars.

# FIFTEEN

# SHILLINGS A WEEK.

*Air :— "King of the Cannibal Islands."*

A MAN and his wife in —— street,
 With seven children young and sweet,
Had a jolly row last night complete,
 About fifteen shillings a week, sir.
He gave his wife a clumsy clout,
Saying, how is all my money laid out,
Tell me quickly he did shout,
And then she soon did set about
Reckoning up without delay,
What she had laid out from day to day,
You shall know what's done, the wife did say,
 With fifteen shillings a week, sir.

Seven children to keep and find in clothes,
And to his wife he did propose,
To reckon how the money goes,
 His fifteen shillings a week, sir.
Threepence-halfpenny a week for milk is
 spent,
One-and-ninepence a week for rent,
For the children a penny for peppermint,
 Out of fifteen shillings a week, sir;
For tobacco eightpence every week,
A half-a-crown for butcher's meat,
And to make your tea complete,
A three-farthing bloater for a treat,
A penny a week for cotton and thread,
Last Sunday, tenpence a small sheep's head,
Ninepence-halfpenny a day for bread,
 Out of fifteen shillings a week, sir.

Potatoes for dinner there must be found,
And there's none for less than a penny a
 pound,
And I must have a sixpenny gown,
 Out of fifteen shillings a week, sir.
A pennorth of starch, a farthing blue,
Twopence-halfpenny soap and potash too,
A ha'porth of onions to make a stew,
Three-halfpence a day small beer for you,
A quartern of butter, sixpennorth of fat,
And to wipe your shoes a twopenny mat,
One halfpenny a day to feed the cat,
 Out of fifteen shillings a week, sir.

Ninepence a week for old dry peas,
Sixpence sugar, eightpence tea,
Pepper, salt, and mustard, farthings three,
 Out of fifteen shillings a week, sir.
One and tenpence-halfpenny, understand,
Every week for firing out of hand,
Threepence-halfpenny candles, a farthing
 sand,
And threepence to bottom the frying-pan;
A twopenny broom to sweep the dirt,
Three-ha'porth of cloth to mend your shirt,
Now don't you think you're greatly hurt,
 Out of fifteen shillings a week, sir.

Clothes for Tommy, Dick, Sal, Polly, and
 Jane,
And Jimmy and Betty must have the same;
You had a sixpenny jacket in Petticoat Lane,
 Out of fifteen shillings a week, sir.
For shaving, a halfpenny twice a week,
A penny to cut your hair so neat,
Threepence for the socks upon your feet,
Last week you bought a tenpenny seat
Besides, old chap, I had most forgot,
You gave a penny for a kidney pie, all hot,
And threepence for an old brown chamberpot,
 Out of fifteen shillings a week, sir.

So now, old chap, you plainly see,
If you can reckon as well as me,
There is little waste in our family,
 Out of fifteen shillings a week, sir.
There's many a woman would think it no sin,
To spend the whole in snuff and gin!
When again to reckon you do begin,
Recollect there's a farthing a week for pins,
To make things right my best I've tried,
That's economy can't be denied.
Dear wife, said he, I'm satisfied,
 Out of fifteen shillings a week, sir.

So you women all the kingdom through,
To you this might appear quite new,
Just see if you the same can do,
 With fifteen shillings a week, sir.

ABOVE: Most things were on sale in the streets. This man is selling fly papers. What would he do in winter?

## SOURCE 183 Experience of a running patterer

From a running patterer, who has been familiar with the trade for many years, I received upwards of a twelvemonth ago, the following statement. After some conversation about 'cocks' [fictions], the most popular of which, my informant said, was the murder at Chigwell-row, he continued:

'That's a trump, to the present day. Why, I'd go out now sir, with a dozen of Chigwell-rows, and earn my supper in half an hour off of 'em. The murder of Sarah Holmes at Lincoln is good, too—that there has been worked for the last five years successively every winter. Poor Sarah Holmes! Bless her! She has saved me from walking the streets all night many a time. Some of the best of these have been in work twenty years—the Scarborough murder has full twenty years. It's called *The Scarborough Tragedy*. I've worked it myself. It's about a noble and rich young naval officer seducing a poor clergyman's daughter. She is confined in a ditch and destroys the child. She is taken up for it, tried and executed. This has had a great run. It sells all round the country places, and would sell now if they had it out. Mostly all our customers is females. They are the chief dependence we have. *The Scarborough Tragedy* is very attractive. It draws tears to the women's eyes to think that a poor clergyman's daughter, who is remarkably beautiful, should murder her own child; it's very touching to every feeling heart. There's a copy of verses with it, too. Then there's *The Liverpool Tragedy*—that's very attractive. It's a mother murdering her own son, through gold . . .

H. Mayhew, *London Labour and the London Poor*, Griffin, 1861, Vol. I, pp. 222-3

## SOURCE 184 Long-song sellers

The long-song sellers did not depend upon patter—though some of them pattered a little—to attract customers, but on the veritable cheapness and novel form in which they vended popular songs, printed on paper rather wider than this page, 'three songs abreast,' and the paper was about a yard long, which constituted the 'three' yards of song. Sometimes three slips were pasted together. The vendors paraded the streets with their 'three yards of new and popular songs' for a penny. The songs are, or were, generally fixed to the top of a long pole, and the vendor 'cried' the different titles as he went along. This branch of 'the profession' is confined solely to the summer . . .

ABOVE: A long-song seller

One man told me that he had cried the following songs in his three yards, and he believed in something like the following order . . .

'I sometimes began,' he said, 'with singing or trying to sing, for I'm no vocalist, the first few words of any song, and them quite loud, I'd begin,

"The Pope he leads a happy life,

He knows no care"—

"Buffalo gals, come out to-night"; "Death of Nelson"; "The gay cavalier"; "Jim along Josey"; "There's a good time coming"; "Drink to me only"; "Kate Kearney"; "Chuckaroo-choo, choo-choo-choot-lah"; "Chockala-roony-ninkaping-nang"; "Pagadaway-dusty-kanty-key"; "Hottypie-gunnypo-china-coo" (that's a Chinese song, sir); "I dreamed that I dwelt in marble halls"; "The standard bearer"; "Just like love"; "Whistle o'er the lave o't"; "Widow Mackree"; "I've been roaming"; "Oh! that kiss"; "The old English gentleman", etc., etc., etc., I dares say they was all in the three yards, or was once, and if they wasn't there was others as good.'

The chief purchasers of the 'long songs' were boys and girls, but mostly boys, who expended 1d. or ½d. for the curiosity and novelty of the things, as the songs were not in the most readable form. A few working people bought them for their children, and some women of the town, who often buy anything fantastic, were also customers.

Mayhew, *London Labour and the London Poor*, Vol. I, p. 221

## The sellers

In 1850 there were probably still several hundred peddlars at work selling broadsides in London alone. Apart from the broadsides they sold they have not left much evidence about themselves. However, a book written by Henry Mayhew called *London Life and the London Poor*, gives us some valuable information about street sellers. Mayhew collected most of his information by interviewing people.

He found that many of the peddlars were strongly independent (source 185):

# THE SENTENCES OF ALL THE PRISONERS,

WHICH COMMENCED ON

## WEDNESDAY,

### 11th Sept., 1822.

BEFORE Justice Hall, Mr Baron Graham, Mr Justice Best, and Mr Justice Richardson, the Lord Mayor, Recorder, and Sheriffs of London, Mr Alderman Ansley, &c.

## IN THE OLD BAILEY.

### DEATH.

Richard Mitford, alias Captain Stracy, for forgery; William Adams for cutting and maiming; William Callaghue, for returning from transportation; Samuel Wilson, Isaac Knight, and James Simpson, for horse-stealing; Samuel Greenwood, John Bridgeman, Robert Ramsey, Thomas Gordon, William Milton, and John Levy, for highway robbery; Thomas Hayes, William Williams, Joseph Williams, Francis Waddel, Mary Gyngell, Daniel Coltrel, John Brown, Walter Blanchard, Alexander Brown, Frank Purdon, William Corbett, alias Watson, Charles Robinson, and Joseph Mackarell, for stealing in dwelling houses; William Reading, for burglary; Edmund Mustoe, James Gardner, William Bright, and George Vergenton, for robbing near the highway; and John Partier, John Roberts, and Stephen Tool, for burglary.

During the time the Recorder was passing sentence of death, the culprits behaved with great propriety. The prisoner, R. Mitford, alias Captain Stracey, for forgery, was attired in a very elegant manner, his youthful and very gentlemanly appearance interested every one present in his lamentable situation. He is the son of a Clergyman.

Holland, King, and North for an unnatural crime.

### TRANSPORTED FOR LIFE.

John Boyle, Cornelius Reading, Joseph Haybury, John Lewis, Thomas Trinder, William Smith, John Strange, and Thomas Harris,

### FOR FOURTEEN YEARS.

Thomas Luby, T. L. Robinson.

### FOR SEVEN YEARS.

William Garrard, Matthew Fennett, James Hicker, James Nicholas Moore, Eliza Davis, David Davis, otherwise Barnard, Rosina Davis, Thomas Long, James Moore, Julia Witherell, Mary Mushton, Christopher Gromer, Edward Fordem, Harriet Wyse, Thomas Jefts, William Needham, Edward Ford, Sarah West, James Harris, George King, Elizabeth Bool, Mary Smith, James Kellerin, William Tuck, John Mackay, George Hilsey, Luke Higgins, Joseph Hunt, George Wiggis, William Jupennan, John Williams, John Card, Hedges, and Willoughby.

——Imprisoned two years, and kept to hard labour.—Thomas Williams, John Pavey, Robert Wilson, John Bankes, and William Tuck, the two latter to be publicly whipped.——Imprisoned one year and kept to hard labour—John Haughton, Joseph Johnson, Joseph Moore, Thomas Letford, Eliza Godfrey, Bridget Callagan, Thomas Burke, and William Coulson,—imprisoned one year in Newgate.—Mary A. L. Butler,—imprisoned six months and kept to hard labour.——Thomas Best, Eleanor Jackson, Mary Barnes, John Hitchen, Sarah Jones, Thomas Griffiths, Eleanor Smith, P. H. Nielle, Ann Hay, Harriet Lee, Richard Spragg, Joseph Thirk, William Jones, James Sidebotham, Thomas Jones, Charles Askew, and James Easthill.

Catherine Rouke, John Gidling, John Wignal, and George Malsby, for felony, to be imprisoned for six months in the House of Correction, and kept to hard labour.—M. Gerard, W. Mayne and M. Pedlard for minor offences, to be fined one shilling and then discharged.—W. Smith and Ann Aldridge for felony, to be imprisoned two months in the House of Correction, and kept to hard labour during that period.—H. Browne, for a felony, to be publicly whipped, and kept to hard labour in the House of Correction for one year.—John Smith and Eliza Lewis, for felonies, to be imprisoned three months in the House of Correction, and kept to hard labour.—T. Worcester and John Jones, for felonies, to be publicly whipped and kept to hard labour for three months in the House of Correction.—Edmund Barber and William Burrell, for a misdemeanour, to be imprisoned six months and kept to hard labour during one month.

Judgment respited on John Parkes, James Hicker, James Nicholas Moore, (whose father is sentenced to transportation) and Thomas Wilbraham.

An immense number were sentenced to various minor periods of imprisonment, some to be publicly and some privately whipped. —— A considerable number were discharged by proclamation.

The number of prisoners tried this Sessions has been between 400 and 500. Adjourned to the 23rd of October.

---

# LAMENTATION OF H. LINGLEY.

Within a dungeon in Norwich gaol,
One Hubbard Lingley in grief bewails,
His own kind uncle he did kill and slay,
On a Friday morning in the month of May.
    For that cruel murder he's doomed to die
    On Norwich fatal sad gallows high.

He is doomed to suffer as I relate
On the very tree where Rush met his fate
In health, in vigour, in youth and bloom,
The murderer Lingley must meet his doom.

In the morning early at four o'clock
He fired a sad and dreadful shot
Which caused his uncle's fatal death wound
Where he fell bleeding upon the ground.

A kind good uncle as may be seen
To his wicked nephew he had been;
Reared him up tenderly and used him well,
And in his cottage with him to dwell.

But he resolved he his blood would spill
His uncle Benjamin he wished to kill;
On Friday morn, the seventeenth of May,
The nephew did his kind uncle slay.

Early in the morning, at four o'clock,
To attract his uncle he fired a shot
And by that spot received the fatal wound.
The murderer flew and left him on the ground

Some labouring men who were passers by,
Saw the murdered in his blood to lie;
Suspicion did on his nephew fall,
And innocent blood did for vengeance call.

Many excuses did Lingley make,
Not having courage to meet his fate;
He before a jury for the deed was tried,
And condemned to suffer on the gallows high.

Hubbard Lingley thought when his uncle died
His place to him would not be denied;
So he was determined to kill and slay,
His uncle dear the seventeenth day of May.

He is doomed to die, nothing can him save,
By the side of Rush in a murderer's grave;
His bones will moulder till the Judgment day,
How could he take his uncle's life away?

At Norwich castle he was tried and cast
And his last moments approaching fast;
The hangman anxious does now await
To terminate Hubbard Lingley's fate.

Oh! all young men a warning take
Think and consider ere it is too late;
How could he dare lift his murderous hand,
Base, vile, ungrateful, and cruel man.

---

ABOVE: This was a standard broadside. The printer would use the same woodcut on similar sheets. All he would then have to do would be to include the relevant information.

The broadside tells us about crime and punishments at this time. Where else would we look for the same information?

ABOVE: Stories about murderers such as Hubbard Lingley were the stock in trade of the running patterers.

Sometimes they invented murders or had the same criminal executed again if they thought the story would sell

ABOVE: Henry Mayhew, printer

## SOURCE 185 Why be a peddlar?

'The innate love of a roving life, which many of the street-people themselves speak of as the cause of their originally taking to the streets, appears to be accompanied by several peculiar characteristics; among the most marked of these are an indomitable "self-will" or hatred of the least restraint or control—an innate aversion to every species of law or government, whether political, moral, or domestic—a stubborn, contradictory nature—an incapability of continuous labour, or remaining long in the same place occupied with the same object, or attending to the same subject—an unusual predilection for amusements, and especially for what partakes of the ludicrous—together with a great relish of all that is ingenious, and so finding extreme delight in tricks and frauds of every kind. There are two patterers now in the streets (brothers)—well-educated and respectably connected—who candidly confess they prefer that kind of life to any other, and would not leave it if they could.'

Mayhew, *London Labour and the London Poor*, Vol. I, p. 214

However, not all the men joined the trade by choice. For some it was a final resort.

## SOURCE 186 Not all by choice

'It was distress that first drove me to it. I had learnt to make willow bonnets, but that branch of trade went entirely out. So, having a wife and children, I was drove to write out a paper that I called "The People's Address to the King on the Present State of the Nation". I got it printed, and took it into the streets and sold it. I did very well with it, and made 5s. a day while it lasted. I never was brought up to any mechanical trade. My father was a clergyman' (here he cried bitterly). 'It breaks my heart when I think of it . . . I would give the world to get out of my present life. It would be heaven to get away from the place where I am.'

Mayhew, *London Labour and the London Poor*, Vol. I, pp. 233-4

# THE POOR LAW CATECHISM.

Q. What is your name?

A. A Pauper.

Q. Who gave you that name?

A. The Board of Guardians, to whom I applied in the time of distress, when first I became a child of want, a member of the workhouse, and an inheritor of all the insults that poverty is heir to.

Q. What did the Board of Guardians do for you.

A. They did promise two things. First, that I should be treated like a convicted felon, being deprived of liberty, and on prison fare. Lastly, that I should be an object of oppression all the days of my life.

Q. Rehearse the Articles of thy belief.

A. I believe in the cruelty of Lord H——y B——m, the author of the present Poor Law, and I also believe that these laws have caused the death of tens of thousands by starvation and neglect.

Q. How many Commandments have you and such as you are to keep?

A. Ten.

Q. Which be they?

A. The same which the Poor Law Commissioners make in Somerset House, saying, We are thy lords and masters, who have caused thee to be confined as in bastiles, and separated thee and the wife of thy bosom, and the children of thy love. 1st, Thou shalt obey no laws but ours. 2nd, Thou shalt not make to thyself any substitute for skilley, nor the likeness of tea, or any other kind of food, or drink, except as is allowed in the workhouse; for we are very jealous men, punishing with severity any transgression against our laws. Should'st thou disobey in this, we shall teach you a lesson that shall last thee all the days of thy life. 3rd, Thou shalt labour hard, and for nothing, and none of thy earnings shall be thy own. 4th, Remember the Sabbath day: six days shalt thou labour hard, and have but little to eat; but the seventh day is the Sabbath, wherein we cannot make you work, and so we give you liberty for an hour or two, to save the parish the expense of your Sunday dinner. 5th. Thou shalt honour the Poor Laws, the Commissioners, and the Beadles; thou shalt take no offence at what they say or do, or else thy days shall be made more miserable in the workhouse wherein thou livest. 6th, Thou shalt commit murder by neglecting thy starving children, for we will give thee no assistance to get them food. 7th, Thou shalt learn to neglect the dear ties of nature, for we will separate thee from the wife of thy bosom, and the children of thy love. 8th, Thou shalt rob thyself of the society and enjoyment of her whom thou hast sworn to protect while life shall last. 9th, Thou shalt be a false witness whenever a Pauper dies, and should the coroner or jury ask you how you live, why tell them you live like lords, and are as happy as princes. 10th, Thou shalt covet all thy neighbour is possessed of, thou shalt covet his friends, his clothes, and all the comforts which thou once had; yet shalt thou long in vain; for remember, oh, pauper! that the motto of every workhouse is—" He who enters here leaves all comforts behind."

## LINES ON THE DEATH OF AN OLD PAUPER.

Oh! Englishmen, come drop a tear or two,
While I relate a thrilling tale of woe,
Of one whose age demanded all the care
That love which aged pilgrims ought to share.
This poor old man, whose limbs refused to bear
The weight of more than eighty years of care,
Was brought before a beak, worse than a Turk,
And sent to gaol because he could not work,
Weep, sons of Britain, mourn your sires' disgrace!
Weep, English mothers! hug your rising race,
And pray to Him, who gave your children breath,

They may not live to die this old man's death,
In a dark dungeon he was close confined,
No friend to comfort, or to soothe his mind;
No child to cheer his loathsome dying bed,
But soon he rested with the silent dead,
Oh, ye who roll in chariots proud and gay,
Ye legal murderers! there will be a day,
When you shall leave all your riches behind,
A dwelling with the ever lost to find,
And your great Master, He whose name is good
Will hold you guilty of your brother's blood.

# Litanies, dialogues and catechisms

Some patterers specialised in 'litanies' or catechisms like the one shown here. Giving a public performance of this type of broadsheet was considered to be difficult and required two men (source 187).

These broadsheets often took the form of propaganda and were usually concerned with religious (often anti-Catholic) or political subjects.

LEFT: This type of broadside was sold after a patterer and an assistant had given a public performance. Religion, politics, and the working of the Poor Law were favourite topics for 'litanies' and 'catechisms', as this type of broadside was called. What do you think was the purpose of this sort of item?

# OLD ENGLAND'S
# BRIGHTEST ORNAMENT

One night at sea while perusing,
And thinking of the time !
I lean'd upon the tiller, and
Composed these few lines,
I thought of men in general,
How they do scheme and plan !
And that England's brightest ornament,
Was the poor hard working man.

### CHORUS.

So cheer up my lads,
Tho' the great may scheme and plan
Old England's brightest ornament,
Is the poor hard working man,

Our miners and our pitmen,
With honours should be crowned;
The richest treasures of the earth,
They bring above the ground,
Do you think that our nobility,
Could toil with Bill or Dan ?
Then why should they look down with scorn,
Upon a working man

Look at our farmer's daughters,
How they will ride in town;
With veils & muffs and crinolines,
And silks and satin gowns.
They go to balls and operas,
And play there with their fan
But quite forget that all these came,
Through the poor hard working man.

I next thought of our navy,
What would old England be?
If it was not for her sailors,
For to guard her on the sea.
Why our British Legislators,
They might scheme and plan ;
But tell me what could they achieve,
But for the Working Man.

The wooden walls of England,
Acknowledged it must be
Are the terror of each tyrant,
And the glory of the sea.
Yet our gentry they command them,
Reap honours and what then ?
They take all the credit that was due,
To the poor hard working man

Our generals in battle,
With spy glass in their hands ;
Will stand upon an eminence,
And issue their commands.
Who is it drubs the enemy,
Who does their jackets tan ;
Why the British private soldier,
For he is the working man.

Our blacksmiths and our foundry men,
O'er blazing fires toil ;
If our aristocracy did this,
Their beauty would spoil.
If they were put in mole skins,
How they themselves would scan;
And think it quite degrading,
For to be a working man.

They say the poor wants knowledge
There work must all be plann'd;
While their betters labour with their heads,
They must toil with their hands.
But if places went by merit,
Deny this fact who can
Why some of England's greatest men,
Would have been a working man.

You working men of England,
Your Maker you exalt ;
So envy not the rich and great,
But forgive them all there faults.
The great supreme created us,
Upon an allwise plan ;
So murmur not because you are,
A poor hard working man.

Before my song is ended,
I've just one word to say ;
For every fair days work we do,
We should get a fair day's pay.
Still let us be contented,
And labour when we can ;
And thank God we are able,
For to be a working Man.

W. FORTH, PRINTER & BOOKBINDER,
63, Waverley Street, Hull.

**16**

## SOURCE 187 Working a litany

To 'work a litany' in the streets is considered one of the higher exercises of professional skill on the part of the patterer. In working this, a clever patterer—who will not scruple to introduce anything out of his head which may strike him as suitable to his audience—is very particular in his choice of a mate, frequently changing his ordinary partner, who may be good 'at a noise' or a ballad, but not have sufficient acuteness or intelligence to patter politics as if he understood what he was speaking about. I am told that there are not twelve patterers in London whom a critical professor of street elocution will admit to be capable of 'working a catachism' or a litany.

'Why, sir,' said one patterer, 'I've gone out with a mate to work a litany, and he's humped it in no time.' To 'hump', in street parlance, is equivalent to 'botch', in more genteel colloquialism. 'And when a thing's humped,' my informant continued, 'you can only "call a go".' To 'call a go,' signifies to remove to another spot, or adopt some other patter, or in short, to resort to some change or other in consequence of a failure.

Mayhew, *London Labour and the London Poor*, Vol. I, p. 236

# Printers

Many towns had at least one printer of broadsides, and some of these men made a lot of money from their trade. Joseph Russell of Birmingham, who issued broadsides between 1818-42, left £12 000 in his will.

The centre of the trade was the Whitechapel area of London where printers like John Pitts and the famous James Catnach operated.

Catnach was the son of a Scottish printer. As a young man he moved from Alnwick in Northumberland to London and started to produce topical items. He specialised in giving the news in verse. When real news was scarce he made it up,

OPPOSITE: Although the broadside comments on the importance of the 'poor hard working man', it is not concerned to suggest changes in society. What was its purpose, do you think?

BELOW LEFT: The East End of London, centre of the nineteenth century broadside printing industry

BELOW: Cheap books came to replace broadsides in popularity. This picture gives a clue to the derivation of the word 'stationer'

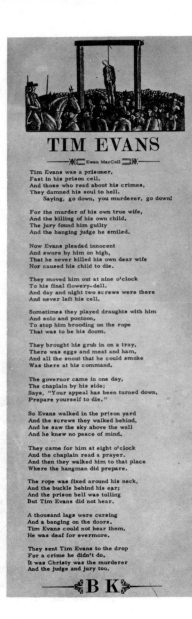

**TIM EVANS**

Ewan MacColl

Tim Evans was a prisoner,
Fast in his prison cell.
And those who read about his crimes,
They damned his soul to hell.
    Saying, go down, you murderer, go down!

For the murder of his own true wife,
And the killing of his own child.
The jury found him guilty
And the hanging judge he smiled.

Now Evans pleaded innocent
And swore by him on high,
That he never killed his own dear wife
Nor caused his child to die.

They moved him out at nine o'clock
To his final flowery-dell.
And day and night two screws were there
And never left his cell.

Sometimes they played draughts with him
And solo and pontoon,
To stop him brooding on the rope
That was to be his doom.

They brought his grub in on a tray,
There was eggs and meat and ham,
And all the snout that he could smoke
Was there at his command.

The governor came in one day,
The chaplain by his side;
Says, "Your appeal has been turned down,
Prepare yourself to die."

So Evans walked in the prison yard
And the screws they walked behind,
And he saw the sky above the wall
And he knew no peace of mind.

They came for him at eight o'clock
And the chaplain read a prayer.
And then they walked him to that place
Where the hangman did prepare.

The rope was fixed around his neck,
And the buckle behind his ear;
And the prison bell was tolling
But Tim Evans did not hear.

A thousand lags were cursing
And a banging on the doors,
Tim Evans could not hear them,
He was deaf for evermore.

They sent Tim Evans to the drop
For a crime he didn't do,
It was Christy was the murderer
And the judge and jury too.

**B K**

and he soon became famous for issuing these 'catchpennies'.

His work was very popular. He is said to have sold two and a half million copies of each of two broadsides dealing with spectacular murders, in 1848 and 1849. He retired to the country a wealthy man.

By about 1860 the broadside press was entering a decline. After the abolition of the stamp duty on newspapers, penny newspapers offered better value. There was also a growing market for cheaply produced books for the mass reading public, and these supplanted old favourites like *The Scarborough Tragedy,* or *Bounce, the Workhouse Beadle,* and *The Examination of the Paupers before the Poor Law Commissioners*.

## Why broadsides are important

The popularity of broadsides shows that they were an important part of everyday life in the first half of the nineteenth century—especially for poorer people. They were entertaining, but songs like *Old England's Brightest Ornament* also gave some people hope and comfort. In some cases, they influenced peoples' attitudes and made them more aware of political matters. They helped to teach deprived people to read, developing literacy among people who could afford neither money for books nor time for education.

They are important for us because they are a significant source of evidence for the early nineteenth century. Some contain important factual information about such things as social conditions of farm labourers and town workers, crime, public events, the working of the Poor Law, political movements and so on.

If you examine the sources used for the other topics in this book, you will find that the majority are from official accounts or records. Broadsides and ballads often give us a view from the other side, the view of ordinary people who were living at the time.

LEFT: Broadsides are alive today. This example printed by John Foreman, 'Broadsheet King', is still in print
RIGHT: What clues are there in this broadside that help you to date it? What conditions are being described and how does it fit in with the section on 'The Vote'?
FAR RIGHT: Religious broadsides were popular. Sometimes they took the form of propaganda like the invitation to Sunday School, or they might offer comfort to people whose lives were hard. Other religious broadsides fell into the class of litanies like the 'Poor Law Catechism' and were often directed against Catholicism, with such titles as 'The Old English Bull John v. The Pope's Bull of Rome'

# SOMETHING TO DO!

## Or a new Touch at the Times.

*(Tune—Chapter of Kings.)*

AS John Bull is disorder'd in heart and in mind,
Since Boney he captur'd, and closely confin'd.
Now the mystery's solv'd, of which Johnny repents,
For our tradesmen can scarcely pay wages and rents.
    Yet barring all pother
    Of this, that, and t'other,
    We only want something to do.

When peace was proclaim'd, trade we thought would revive,
And Old England, once more, be again all alive;
But war is the theme some would gladly pursue,
For while we were fighting we'd plenty to do.
    For working or fighting,
    When we take delight in,
    'Tis because we want something to do.

As Reform is the wish of each Englishman's heart,
Which, peaceably gain'd, would its blessings impart;
Relieve the mechanic—assuage all his woes,
And industry furnish meat, money, and clothes.
    Were that system pursu'd,
    And our commerce renew'd,
    We should all then have plenty to do.

Some preach up equality's frivolous plan,
And other chimeras, most foreign to man;
But if that vile fashion but once did prevail,
We should all want to drink—but pray who'd brew the ale?
    But each in his station
    Is best for the nation,
    As we only want something to do.

Of American freedom some patriots boast,
And hundreds are shipp'd ev'ry year from our coast;
But no sooner get there than they cry out 'Alack!'
And wish themselves *safe* aye and *speedily* back.
    For the Yankies now find,
    If to Englishmen kind,
    They themselves may want something to do.

That John Bull is industrious none can deny,
If he can but get beef-steaks and onions to fry;
But, if working won't do, he begins for to grunt,
And he goes a reforming with Moorhouse and Hunt.

But the soldiers, with s,ears,
Caught poor Johnny's ears,
While waiting for something to do.

Should commerce revive, and all hands in employ,
All declaimers would cease, then, his peace to annoy;
Contented in mind, and a better fill'd purse,
He takes all rubs gently for better or worse.
    But when nothing's doing,
    John's mind is a brewing
    Some mischief for something to do.

The distress'd manufacturers sorely complain
Of taxes and poor-rates, of heavy distrain;
So that master and man, in the general strife,
Are bother'd and plagu'd all the days of their life.
    What with large stocks on hand,
    And but little demand,
    They are all wanting something to do.

In the general contention we hear little said
Of placemen and pensioners squabbling for bread;
They hire needy fellows to do all their work,
And awe them, forsooth, with the frown of a Turk.
    Your snug sinecures
    No Briton endures,
    Whose fingers want something to do.

As our statesmen economy laudably preach,
But its *practice* contrive so neat to o'erreach;
That their words and their actions belie the **report**
That economy's ever subscrib'd to at court.
    For they're ever contriving,
    And always conniving,
    At something—for nothing to do.

May the blessings of commerce again cheer our isle,
And each honest man on his face wear a smile;
Our laws and our church be rever'd as they ought,
And supporters of anarchy set quite at naught.
    As for them and their cause,
    Give them both to the laws,
    We merely want something to do.

*Swindells, Printer, Manchester.*

---

# Happy DAY.

## INVITATION TO SUNDAY SCHOOLS.

Sold by R. Barr, 72, Marsh Lane, Leeds.

I'm glad I ever saw the day,
We ever met to sing and pray:
I've glory, glory in my soul,
Which makes me praise the Lord so bold.

### CHORUS.

Happy day, Happy day,
When Jesus took my sins away,
He taught me how to watch and pray,
And live rejoicing every day,
Happy day, Happy day,
When Jesus washed my sins away.

I hope to praise him when I die,
And shout Salvation as I fly,
Sing glory, glory glory through the air,
And meet my father's children there.
    *Happy day, &c.*

Take my poor heart and let it be,
For ever closed to all but thee,
Seal thou my breast and let me wear,
That pledge of love for ever there.
    *Happy day, &c.*

Praise God for what he's done for me,
Once I was blind but now I see,
I on the brink of ruin fell,
Glory to God I'm out of hell.
    *Happy day, &c.*

Come sinners come along with us,
For there is room in thet blest house;
Repent, believe for holiness,
And you shall go and sing with us
    *Happy day, &c.*

O come, come away,—
From labour now reposing,
Let anxious care awhile forbear;
    O come, come away,
Who does not wish to die a fool
Must early come to Sunday School,
And learn the Saviour's rule,
    So come, come away.

O come, come away,—
The Sabbath day's returned,
Which calls on all to come to School,
    So come, come away,
Your Teachers then with joy shall know
You wish to taste those joys below,
Which Christians only know,
    So come, come away.

O come, come away,
Let's search the sacred treasure,
Which David said would not mislead,
    O come, come away,—
Such toil will gain its own reward,
In blessings from our gracious Lord,
For faithful is his word,
    So come, come away.

Then come, come away,—
The glorious is dawning,
When Christians all both great and small,
    Shall cry come away,
Come take your palms through Jesus won
And hail the saviour on his throne,
And shout the work is done,
    So come, come away.

# Glossary

**able-bodied poor**   those poor people considered fit and capable of working

**accrued**   resulted

**acquitted**   found not guilty

**aggregate**   total amount

**amanuensis**   secretary

**amelioration**   improvement of conditions

**annihilated**   wiped out

**apoplexy**   a fit affecting the brain and resulting in loss of sensation and movement

**apprehension**   fear

**artisans**   skilled craftsmen

**authentic**   genuine

**aversion**   dislike

**barbarism**   total lack of culture and civilisation

**beneficial**   good, helpful

**borough**   a town with a corporation and privileges conferred by royal charter

**broadsides**   sheets of paper with songs printed on one side, used for spreading news and propaganda

**burgageholds**   an ancient form of tenure of property

**cant**   meaningless language, slogans

**canvassing**   trying to persuade other people to accept your case

**celerity**   speed

**charismatic**   compelling, holding an almost divine fascination for others

**chastise**   punish

**Commissioners**   those appointed to serve on a Royal Commission and prepare a Report for the government after investigating a particular topic

**commodities**   all the things necessary to life, such as food, clothes, household goods

**compensate**   make up for

**concourse**   crowd

**concur**   agree

**conducive**   encouraging, helpful

**constitution**   rules for governing the country

**consummation**   completion

**contemporaries**   people alive at the time

**contested**   elections which were fought by the representatives of different parties

**conveyance**   transportation

**Corn Law 1815**   an attempt to protect the farmers from the effects of the falling price of corn and competition from cheap imported corn. 80 shillings a quarter was taken as the lowest selling price that would give the producing farmer a reasonable profit, and when the price fell below this level, the ports would be closed to the importation of foreign corn. When it rose above 80 shillings, the ports would be open to free importation

**delegates**   elected to represent others at a conference or meeting

**derangements**   breakdowns

**detour**   way round

**diabolical**   evil, devil-like

**diligence**   persistent hard work

**disapprobation**   disapproval

**dissenting**   belonging to protestant sects separated from the established Church of England

**dissolution**   disintegration

**eminently**   obviously

**emporium**   shop, general store

**erratic**   uncertain, irregular

**erroneous**   mistaken

**expedited**   speeded up

**fabrication**   manufacture

**facilitate**   make easy

**fiasco**   complete and utter failure

**fluctuations**   variations, rise and fall

**formidable portion**   staggeringly huge part

**franchise**   the right to vote at elections

**freehold**   unconditional ownership of property for life

**Freeman**   a citizen of a borough who, through inheritance, marriage, nomination, apprenticeship or purchase, was allowed, in mediaeval times, to hold municipal office, vote in parliamentary elections and engage in trade as a master. By the eighteenth century the Freemen of many cities had become a self-perpetuating oligarchy. They excluded other citizens from having any say in the affairs of the borough and governed it in their own interests. Often, they did not even live there

**gratifying**   pleasing

**habitual**   regular, continual

**hamlet**   tiny village or settlement

**hustings**   platform from which candidates for Parliament were nominated

**huzzahs**   applause, cries of encouragement, cheers

**impious**   wicked

**incumbent**   holder of religious office, such as a vicar or curate

**indomitable**   impossible to crush

**inducements**   attractions

**inhabitants at large**   all the people living in the place

**iniquities**   evils, wickedness

**innate**   inborn

**insurgents**   rebels

**intemperance**   excessive drinking

**intercourse**   movement

**leasehold**   conditional possession of property, the leaseholder having to pay rent according to a contract with the owner

**litany**    questions and answers according to the pattern of church services

**Luddites**    the Luddites were a Nottinghamshire band of daring and desperate men, led by Ned Ludd. They fought back against the threats to their livelihoods posed by the new practice of cutting up cloth knitted on wide frames and making it into garments which sold for less than those knitted on proper narrow frames. The Luddite campaign began in the spring of 1811 and the Luddites smashed the wide frames in villages all over the county. Later, gangs of men in other parts of the country who smashed up new machinery which threatened to make skilled craftsmen redundant were given the name Luddites too

**ludicrous**    ridiculous

**Magna Carta of their motive freedom**    giving them the right and freedom to travel to other parts of the country for the first time

**mercantile**    merchants, traders

**metropolis**    the largest city of a region or country, in this case London

**metropolitan**    belonging to or characteristic of a metropolis

**mettle**    (to do) one's best

**monopoly**    sole ownership of a trade

**myriads**    uncountable numbers

**nonconformists**    those belonging to protestant sects outside the Church of England

**nominee**    someone appointed by another person to do a job

**oakum**    loose fibre obtained by picking old rope to pieces

**ordinances**    rites or services laid down by a religion

**parlance**    jargon, language

**partisans**    supporters

**paupers**    people with no means of supporting themselves at all

**pecuniary**    financial

**peers**    the aristocracy—dukes, marquises, earls, viscounts and barons

**philanthropists**    people who love others and do charitable work on their behalf

**potwallopers**    those who were masters of their own fireplaces and the pot on their hearth, or who held the key to their own doors

**predilection**    preference

**privation**    lack of the comforts and necessities of life

**procure**    obtain

**prodigious**    enormous

**propriety**    wisdom

**prostrate**    humble

**provincial**    in the provinces, outside London

**pugilist**    fighter

**radical**    someone who wants to change fundamentally the existing order of things

**redundant**    no longer needed for work, unemployed

**remedy**    repair

**repressed**    kept down

**revolutionary**    person who works actively to overthrow the existing political system by force

**salutary**    beneficial, producing good effects

**satirical**    sarcastic, humorously critical

**scot and lot**    the right to vote was based on the payment of certain small municipal taxes

**seditious**    agitation directed against the state, speech or behaviour encouraging rebellion

**segregation**    separation

**sinecure**    a job with pay but no duties

**specie**    corn as opposed to paper money

**sporadic**    intermittent

**staple**    main, chief

**suffrages**    votes

**temporal**    earthly, of this life

**tenements**    dwellings, living apartments

**theological controversies**    arguments about religion

**tithes**    taxes paid by parishioners to support the church and clergy, usually in the form of one tenth of their farm produce, and work on the church's land

**tolls**    fees charged

**Tories**    members of a party which emerged in the late seventeenth century. Traditionally, they supported Crown and established church. They opposed the Whigs (see below)

**tranquillised**    made quiet

**tribulation**    suffering

**trump**    the most profitable stroke of luck

**turnpike trusts**    companies set up to finance the building and maintenance of roads

**unanimously**    without any opposition

**unappropriated**    not owned or claimed by anyone

**unenfranchised**    not allowed to vote

**uniformity**    the same everywhere

**urban**    in the towns and cities

**vended**    sold

**veritable**    real

**vested**    given to, conferred on

**vested rights**    possession of rights to property

**vilified**    abused, spoken ill of

**vis à vis**    type of carriage in which people sit facing each other

**void**   invalid, without legal force

**weal**   welfare

**Whigs**   members of a political party which first emerged in the late seventeenth century. In 1845, the Whigs stood for the principles of free trade (no duties), Catholic emancipation (full rights for Catholics like everyone else), the reduction of Crown patronage (particularly the giving out of sinecures) and the reform of the electoral system. The Whigs wanted to give the right to vote to more people, they regarded the existing system as unfair because it was so out of date. They also wanted the growing industrial towns to be better represented in Parliament

**wrought**   engaged in physical work

**zealous**   keen, dedicated and earnest

# Bibliography

**Acworth, W. M.,** The Railways of England, Murray, 1899

**Alison, M.D., R. Scott,** 'Report on the sanitary conditions of Tranent, and neighbouring district at Haddingtonshire', Parliamentary Papers, Lords, 1842, Vol. XXVII, in E. Royston Pike (ed.), Human Documents of the Industrial Revolution, Allen & Unwin, 1970

**Ashwell, A. R.,** Life of the Right Reverend Samuel Wilberforce, London, 1880-82 (source 122)

**Aspinall, A.** (ed.), Letters of George IV, Oxford University Press, 1938

**Aspinall, A. & Smith, E. A.** (eds.), English Historical Documents 1783-1832, Eyre & Spottiswoode, 1959 (sources 5, 11)

**Bamford, Samuel,** Passages in the Life of a Radical, Simpkin, 1844

**Birley, Joseph,** Sadler's Bill, 1832

**Brown, John,** A Memoir of Robert Blincoe, 1832

**Brydone, James Marr,** Narrative of a voyage ... to Toronto, Upper Canada, 1834

**Burnett, John,** Plenty and Want, Penguin Books, 1968

**Civil Engineer, A,** Personal Recollections of English Engineers, 1868

**Clark, C. M.** (ed.), Select Documents in Australian History, International Publication Service, 1970

**Cochrane, Thomas, Earl of Dundonald,** Autobiography of a Seaman, London, 1861

**Cole, G. D. H. & Filson, A. W.,** British Working Class Movements, Macmillan, 1967 (sources 24, 32, 65, 66)

**Cooper, Thomas,** The Life, written by himself, London, 1872

**Corder, S.,** Life of Elizabeth Fry, London, 1853

**Dawson, K. & Wall, P.,** The Problem of Poverty, Oxford University Press, 1969 (source 90)

**Dickens, Charles,** Oliver Twist, London, 1838

**Eden, F. M.,** The State of the Poor, London, 1797

**Finer, S. E.,** The Life and Times of Sir Edwin Chadwick, Methuen, 1952

'First Annual Report of the Poor Law Commissioners', 1835

**Flinn, M. W.,** Readings in Economic and Social History, Macmillan, 1965 (source 163)

**Francis, Beata & Keary, Eliza** (eds.), The Francis Letters, London, 1901

**Francis, J.,** A History of the English Railway, Longman, 1851

**Gammage, R. G.,** History of the Chartist Movement, Newcastle-on-Tyne, 1894 (sources 33, 93)

**Glen, W. C.,** The Statutes in Force Relating to the Poor, London, 1857

**Glyde, John,** The Moral, Social and Religious Condition of Ipswich, 1850, S. R. Publishers, 1971 edition

**Gray, T.,** Observations on a General Iron Rail-way, Baldwin, 1823

**Grego, Joseph,** A History of Parliamentary Elections and Electioneering, Chatto, 1886 (source 10)

**Gurney, Joseph,** Notes on a visit made to some of the Prisons in Scotland and the North of England in company with Elizabeth Fry, Longman, 1819

**Harrison, J. F. C.,** The Early Victorians, 1832-51, Weidenfeld & Nicolson, 1968

**Helps, A.,** The Life and Labours of Mr. Brassey, 1805-1870, London, 1872

**Hill, Rowland,** The State and Progress of Penny Postage, Charles Knight, 1844

**Hobsbawm, E. J. & Rude, G.,** Captain Swing, Lawrence & Wishart, 1970

**Hodder, E.,** The Life and Work of the seventh Earl of Shaftesbury, London, 1887

**Hunt, Henry,** The Green Bag Plot, 1819

**Inglis, K. S.,** Churches and the Working Classes in Victorian England, Routledge & Kegan Paul, 1969 (sources 128, 131)

**Innis, H. A. & Lower, A. R.** (eds.), Select Documents in Canadian Economic History 1783-1855, Toronto, 1933

**Jackman, W. T.,** The Development of Transportation in Modern England, Cambridge University Press, 1916 (source 166)

**Jennings, L. J.** (ed.), Correspondence and Diaries of John Wilson Croker, London, 1884

**King, Rev. John,** The Cholera, God's Sore Judgement on the Nations of the Earth, 1849

**Knowles, George,** 'Observations in the Expediency of Making a Line of Railroad from York to Scarborough', in E. W. Martin (ed.), Country Life in England, Macdonald, 1966

**Lewis, G. King,** Elizabeth Fry, London, 1910

**Macturk, G. G.,** A History of the Hull Railways, Hull, 1879

**Malmesbury, Lord,** *Memoirs of an Ex-Minister,* Longman, 1885

**Malthus, Rev. T. R.,** *An Essay on the Principle of Population,* London, 1798

**Martin, E. W.** (ed.), *Country Life in England,* Macdonald, 1966

**Masterman, C. F. G.,** *Frederick Denison Maurice,* London & Oxford, 1907

**Mayhall, John,** *Annals of Leeds, York and the Surrounding District,* 1865

**Mayhew, H.,** *London Labour and the London Poor,* Griffin, 1861

**Mitchell, B. R. & Deane, P.,** *Abstract of British Historical Statistics,* Cambridge University Press, 1971

**Morris, M.** (ed.), *From Cobbett to the Chartists,* Lawrence & Wishart, 1948 (source 62)

**Oastler, R.,** *The Right of the Poor to Liberty and Life,* Liverpool, 1838

**O'Connor, T. P.,** *Memoirs,* Benn, 1929

Offences and Punishment Book of Newry Workhouse', Northern Ireland Record Office

**Palmer, R.** (ed.), *The Painful Plough,* Cambridge University Press, 1973

**Parsons, H.,** *The Tourists' Companion,* 1834

**Perkin, H.,** *The Origins of Modern English Society 1780-1880,* Routledge & Kegan Paul, 1969 (source 129)

**Pike, E. Royston** (ed.), *Human Documents of the Industrial Revolution,* Allen & Unwin, 1970 (source 105)

**Pollins, H.,** *Britain's Railways,* David & Charles, 1971

**Porter, G. R.,** *The Progress of the Nation,* H. Bohn, 1838

**Prentice, Archibald,** *Historical Sketches and Personal Recollections of Manchester intended to illustrate the progress of public opinion from 1792 to 1832,* London, 1851

'Report into the Administration and Practical Operation of the Poor Laws', 1834

'Report of Select Committee on the Health of Towns', *Parliamentary Papers,* 1840, Vol. XI

'Report of the Further Amendment of the Poor Law', 1839

Report of the Royal Commission into the Poor Laws', 1834, 1905 edition

Report of the Secret Committee of the House of Commons on the disturbed state of the country', 19 February 1817, *Parliamentary Debates,* XXXV

Report of the Select Committee on the Andover Union', 1846

**Rose, M. E.,** *The English Poor Law,* David & Charles, 1971 (sources 68, 75, 84, 89)

'Second Annual Report of the Poor Law Commissioners', 1837

**Smiles, Samuel,** *Self-Help,* London, 1859

**Smiles, Samuel,** *Story of the Life of George Stephenson,* Murray, 1862 (source 148)

**Sockett, Rev. T.** (ed.), *Letters from Sussex Emigrants,* 1832

**Solway, R. A.,** *Prelates and People, 1783-1852,* Routledge & Kegan Paul, 1968

**Stanley, A. P.** *et al., Sermons Preached to Working People,* Macmillan, 1867

**Strachey, L. & Fulford, R.** (eds.), *The Greville Memoirs,* Macmillan, 1938

**Summer, J. B.,** *A Charge delivered to the Clergy of the Diocese of Chester,* Hatchard, 1838

**Sykes, John,** *Local Records or Historical Register of remarkable events which have occurred in Northumberland and Durham,* Newcastle, 1866

**Tames, R.,** *Railways,* Oxford University Press, 1970 (source 180)

**Taylor, W. Cooke,** *Notes of a Tour of the Manufacturing Districts of Lancashire,* 1842

Third Annual Report of the Poor Law Commissioners', 1837

**Thorp, Rev. T.,** *Individual Vice, Social Sin,* 1832

**Tonna, C. E.,** *The Perils of the Nation,* 1844

**West, Julius,** *A History of the Chartist Movement,* Constable, 1920 (source 4)

**Wilberforce, Samuel,** *A Charge Delivered to the Clergy of The Archdeaconry of Surrey,* London, 1844

**Young, G. M. & Handcock, W. D.** (eds.), *English Historical Documents 1833-74.* Eyre & Spottiswoode, 1956 (sources 168, 172)

Contemporary journals and newspapers referred to in sources:
*Chartist Circular*
*The Economist*
*Hull Advertiser*
*Illustrated London News*
*Leeds Mercury*
*Northern Liberator*
*Northern Star*
*The Poor Man's Guardian*
*Quarterly Review*
*Railway Times*
*The Scotsman*
*The Times*
*Weekly Political Register*
*The Weekly Record*

# Acknowledgements

The authors and publishers are grateful to the following for permission to reproduce copyright material:

**Photographs and illustrations**

Front cover *Picnic at Ascot, 1843*, Mansell Collection; page 6 *Leeds c. 1815*, Mansell Collection; page 7 *'State of the nation' cartoon*, By courtesy of the Trustees of the British Museum, BM 15799; page 8 *Samuel Bamford*, City of Manchester Cultural Services, Local History Library; page 9 *Rotten boroughs*, Mary Evans Picture Library; page 10 *Votes advertisement*, Hull Public Libraries; page 11 *Candidate winning votes (cartoon)*, Radio Times Hulton Picture Library, *Cartoon by Cruickshank*, Mansell Collection; page 12 *Phiz cartoon* and *Election ball*, Mansell Collection; page 14 *Thomas Cochrane, Earl Dundonald*, Mansell Collection; page 16 *'Death or liberty' cartoon*, Trustees of the British Museum, BM 13279; page 17 *Earl Fitzwilliam*, Mansell Collection, *Peterloo Massacre*, Radio Times Hulton Picture Library; page 18 *One view of freedom of speech*, Trustees of the British Museum, BM 13287; page 19 *Archibald Prentice*, Manchester Local History Library; page 20 *Cartoon*, Trustees of the British Museum, BM 16610, *Thomas Attwood*, Radio Times Hulton Picture Library; page 21 *Bristol riots*, Mary Evans Picture Library; page 23 *George IV*, Mansell Collection; page 26 *page from 'The Poor Man's Guardian', 1832*; page 27 *William Lovett*, Radio Times; page 28 *Feargus O'Connor*, Radio Times, page 29 *A Charter party*, from 'Cruickshank, Comic Almanac, 1843*; *Newport Riots*, Radio Times; page 31 *Thomas Cooper*, Radio Times, *Chartist meeting at Kennington*, Mansell Collection; page 33 *Chartist cartoon*, Mansell Collection; page 34 *William Thompson*, Sunderland Museum and Art Gallery, *Viscount Howick cartoon*, Radio Times; page 35 *Sunderland c. 1840*, Sunderland Museum and Art Gallery; page 36 *Wolverley Attwood*, Sunderland Museum and Art Gallery; pages 37, 38, 40, 41, *Handbills*, Department of Palaeography and Diplomatic, Durham University; page 43 *The Thompson Arms Hotel*, Sunderland Museum and Art Gallery; page 45 *Vouchers*, Durham University; page 46 *Evening at the opera*, Mansell Collection; page 47 *London slum*, Mansell Collection; page 48 *Scottish emigrants*, Radio Times; page 49 *Christmas dinner*, Mansell Collection; page 50 *Irish hovel* and *Northumberland cottages*, Mansell Collection; page 51 *Nut-meg grater seller*, Mayhew, *London Life*; page 53 *Machine wreckers*, Mansell Collection; page 54 *Robert Owen*, and *Over-population cartoon*, Mansell Collection; page 57 *Bread riots*, Mary Evans Picture Library; page 58 *New Lanark Mills*, Mansell Collection; page 59 *Cartoon on Owen*, Mansell Collection; page 61 *Cartoon*, Mansell Collection; page 62 *Sir Edwin Chadwick*, Radio Times; page 63 *Swing, the rick-burner*, and *The Swing catcher*, Mansell Collection; page 65 *Mob burning farm*, Mary Evans Library; page 66 *Workhouse dietary*, Hull Public Libraries, *Women's yard in a workhouse*, Radio Times; page 67 *Scarborough workhouse*, Mary Evans Library; page 68 *Workhouse dinner*, Radio Times, *Cobbling class*, Mary Evans Library; page 69 *Women's quarters*, Mansell Collection; page 70 *Dr Guthrie's ragged school*, Mansell Collection; page 72 *Richard Oastler*, Radio Times; page 73 *J. R. Stephens*, Radio Times; page 74 *Mother and child*, Mary Evans Library; page 78 *Irish peasants*, Radio Times; page 79 *Stone breaking*, Mansell Collection; page 80 *Depopulation cartoon*, Cruickshank; page 83 *Emigrants*, Mary Evans Library; page 85 *List of necessaries*, from the Lord Egremont Collection in the Petworth House Archives, West Sussex Records Office; page 86 *'Bourneuf' ship plan*, Mary Evans Library; page 87 *Scale of victualling*, West Sussex Records Office; page 88 *Emigrants departing* and *Emigrants on deck*, Mansell ... Collection; page 89 *Medical inspection*, Radio Times; page 91 *Emigrants at work*, Mansell Collection; page 92 *Shanty in the Bush*, Radio Times; page 93 *Prosperous estate*, Mansell Collection; page 94 *Houses in Wolverhampton*, Wolverhampton Public Libraries; page 96 *A court for King Cholera*, Mansell Collection; page 99 *Brick making*, Radio Times; page 100 *Cheap clothing cartoon*, Radio Times; page 101 *Down and outs*, from Dore's *London*; page 102 *Samuel Wilberforce*, Radio Times; page 103 *Christmas at church*, Mansell Collection; page 105 *Churchgoing in the 1830s*, Mary Evans Library; page 106 *Sweeping up children cartoon*, Radio Times; page 107 *Soup kitchen in Coventry*, Radio Times; page 108

*Methodist preaching*, Mary Evans Library; page 109 *F. D. Maurice*, Mansell Collection; page 110 *Bible reading*, from Dore, *Mission to seamen*, Radio Times; page 111 *Lord Shaftesbury*, Radio Times; page 112 *Ragged school prize giving*, Radio Times; page 113 *Women prisoners*, Mansell Collection; page 115 *Elizabeth Fry*, Radio Times; page 116 *Convicts exercising*, Radio Times; page 117 *Oakum picking*, Mansell Collection; page 118 *Trevithick's Racing Steam Horse*, from a watercolour by T. P. Rowlandson, print courtesy of the Science Museum, London; page 119 *Wagon ways*, Radio Times; page 120 *George Stephenson*, Mansell Collection, *Opening of the Stockton–Darlington railway*, Radio Times; page 122 *Olive Mount cutting*, Mansell Collection; pages 124, 125 *Travelling on the Liverpool–Manchester line*, Science Museum, London; page 127 *Brunel*, Radio Times; page 128 *Hudson*, Radio Times; page 130 *Thomas Brassey*, Mary Evans Library; page 131 *Blasting a tunnel*, Mansell Collection, *Newspaper advertisement*, reproduced from the Local History Collection in the Hull Central Library by kind permission of the Director of Leisure Services, Humberside County Council; page 132 *A navvy*, Mansell Collection; page 133 *Making a cutting*, Science Museum; page 134 *A railway navvies' camp*, Leicestershire Museums' Newton Collection; page 136 *Construction work at Blackfriars*, Mary Evans Library; page 137 *carriages on the Liverpool–Manchester line*, Mansell Collection; page 138 *Break of gauge at Gloucester*, Mary Evans Library, *'Punch' cartoon*, Mansell Collection; page 143 *Swindon*, British Rail Board; page 144 *Crewe fete*, Mary Evans Library; page 145 *Scarborough poster*, from G. Fowkes, *Railway History and the Local Historian*, E. Yorks Local History Society; page 147 *Unemployed coachmen cartoon*, Mansell Collection; page 148 *Railway guard*, Mary Evans Library; page 149 *Excursions cartoon*, Mansell Collection; page 150 *Newcastle engineering works*, Mary Evans Library; page 152 *Frost Fair*, Mansell Collection; page 153 *Broadside*, Bradford Public Libraries; page 154 *Broadside ('Manchester')*, Bradford Public Libraries, *Broadside ('Fifteen shillings a week')*, from C. Hindley, *Curiosities of Street Literature*, Seven Dials Press; page 155 *Fly-paper seller*, from Dore; page 156 *Long song seller*, Mansell Collection; page 157 *Broadsides*, from C. Hindley, *Curiosities of Street Literature*; page 158 *Henry Mayhew*, from H. Mayhew, *London Life and the London Poor, 1861*; page 160 *Broadside* Bradford Public Libraries; page 161 *Street stationer*, Mansell Collection; page 162 *Tim Evans*, courtesy of John Foreman, Broadsheet King; page 163 *Broadsides*, Bradford Public Libraries; Back cover *'The kitchen'*, Radio Times Hulton Picture Library;

**Extracts**

Sources 5, 11, 16, 28, 168, 172, Associated Book Publishers Ltd; source 7, Ernest Benn Ltd; sources 24, 30, 32, 37, 60, 65, 66, 163, Macmillan Publishers Ltd; source 52, by permission of Professor John Burnett; sources 57, 76, Methuen & Co. Ltd; sources 62, 71, 72, Lawrence & Wishart Ltd; sources 68, 75, 84, 89, David & Charles; sources 105, 178, George Allen & Unwin Ltd; source 111, Weidenfeld & Nicolson Ltd; sources 116, 117, 127, 128, 129, 131, Routledge & Kegan Paul Ltd; source 152, Macdonald and Jane's Ltd; sources 166, 170, Cambridge University Press Ltd; source 182, George G. Harrap & Company Ltd.